IN THE ZONE

IN THE ZONE

Living a Life in God's Blessings

PATRICIA KING

Unless otherwise identified, Scripture quotations are from the New American Standard Bible®, Copyright © 1960,1962,1963,1968,1971,1972,1973,1975,1977,1995 by The Lockman Foundation. Used by permission.

Scripture quotations marked KJV are from the King James Version.

Published by XP Publishing
A department of Christian Services Association
P.O. Box 1017
Maricopa, Arizona 85139
www.XPpublishing.com

Printed in Canada

ISBN: 978-1-936101-00-9

DEDICATION

Dedicated to
Kenneth Copeland,
who through his anointed teachings
instructed me as a young believer
to live in covenant blessing.

ENDORSEMENTS

I just finished reading Patricia's *In the Zone*. Wow! It's chock full of Scripture and completely permeated with insight, discernment and godly wisdom as it relates to entering that "Zone" where you and the Godhead can interact and experience encouragement and victory together! There are so many adjectives I could use. The chapter on FAVOR is worth the whole book. But so are the chapters on BLESSING and LOVE and all the others. You'll experience what it means, perhaps more than ever, to make DECREES over your life in these many areas. This book was just what I needed to read and it was also just WHEN I needed to read it. It is like a "how-to" book to get truth off the pages of the written Word of God, and then how to get these truths into your head; but most importantly how to get them once and for all INTO YOUR HEART where you'll get into THE ZONE. I don't think you'll ever be the same!

STEVE SCHULTZ
The Elijah List

There is a dwelling place in God where He abides in us as we abide in Him. In that place, all things are possible! There is no place like that place and there is no other place I want to be in. How about you? Do you want to learn what you were created for? *In The Zone* you learn about the power of God's blessing, how to please God, how to be positioned for your next blessing and so much more. Come on now – let's get *In The Zone* together and be blessed to be a blessing!

JAMES W. GOLL
Encounters Network • Prayer Storm • Compassion Acts
Author of *The Seer, The Lost Art of Intercession,
Dream Language, Empowered Prayer* and others.

Patricia King's new book *In The Zone* is a call to the body of Christ to rise up into the dimension of abundance that God has made available for us all. It contains an important message for "such a time as this" as we learn how to trust in the Lord and lean not on our own understanding. You will be blessed and feel the impartation of the Holy Spirit leading you into the glory as you read this book.

JOSHUA MILLS
New Wine International

In the Zone is a book every Christian should read at least twice a year. This will allow us to test what Zone we are presently living in and make adjustments, if necessary, to bring us back to the place of blessing which is ours by inheritance. Patricia King openly and aptly shares her own testimony of finding a "permanent place of victory through standing on the Word of God with unshakable faith" and learning to live there. She does not rely on her experiences to substantiate the truth of the book, but gives numerous Scriptures to support the reality and possibility of it.

"When you live in THE ZONE, everything turns into a blessing" (Pg.60). If you are longing for God's favor upon your life, if you have a sense of being unfulfilled in spite of your many prayers, this book is for you. Read it with an open heart and it will help you understand the empty feelings you may have, teach you how to step beyond them and walk into another "Zone." You will learn that both your longing for something more and the fulfillment of that are from God.

IVERNA M. TOMPKINS, DD
Scottsdale, Arizona

Rarely have I met a person who lives as deeply *In the Zone* as Patricia King. This book is not mere words, it is a testimony of the power of God as Patricia has known it and lived it at many levels: in faith, favor, blessings (even the ones in disguise) – and many other aspects of God's glory. You will be inspired to go deeper into your destiny as you read this great book."

STACEY CAMPBELL
www.revivalnow.com
www.beahero.org

Patricia King has written an outstanding faith-building dynamic book that can revolutionize your life and bring you into God's abundant blessing. I encourage everyone to read *In the Zone*. This is a book that you will want to read over and over again.

CHE AHN
Senior Pastor, Harvest Rock Church
President of Harvest International Ministry

I love Patricia King's new book *In the Zone*! During a time of great shaking in the world around us it is a now word from the Lord on how to live in the supernatural realm of God's blessing. It is filled with eternal truths as well as real life examples on how to live an upgraded life where you can receive every good thing God has for you. Your faith will soar to new heights as you gain keys that will release God's favor, abundance, provision, healing, and permanent victory in every area of your life. Get ready to have your deepest pain transformed into your greatest promotion! This book will propel you into the Zone where you will be completely overtaken by God's blessing and goodness.

MATT SORGER
Host of TV's Power for Life
Matt Sorger Ministries

In the Zone is a refreshing and life-changing devotional. By highlighting the finished work of the Cross, Patricia shares powerful truths from heaven's point of view. Each faith-building page is chock full of insights and practical Word applications that will help you firmly grasp who you really are in Christ and show you how to recognize today's impossibilities as the makings for tomorrow's miracles. I heartily recommend that you study this book thoroughly from cover to cover, giving each revelation plenty of time to sink in. The stunning implications of living life "In the Zone" of lavish love and abundant blessings are endless for you and your family, and will be found completely irresistible by the world around you as you hold out life and hope to them.

GEORGIAN BANOV
President and Co-Founder of Global Celebration

You will love this new book by Patricia King, *In The Zone*. There is a level of faith that jumps right into you as you read the written words on the pages. It is as if every word were prayed over and an impartation takes place that draws you into a deeper faith. I found myself saying, "Yes, this is mine. This is mine." Patricia embodies Mark 10:13-16. She accepts the Word of God with the faith of a child. She knows it is hers and she invites everyone else along for the journey. She goes after the extreme in God and God shows up in extreme ways. Her faith and love for Jesus and joy in the journey are contagious. This is the very experience I had while reading this manuscript and meditating on the passages of Scriptures that she shares. I invite you to get into *The Zone,* and I believe you will find yourself knowing and declaring every morning, "Today...I am IN THE ZONE...TODAY this is mine..." just like I do.

JULIE MEYER
International House Of Prayer

CONTENTS

FOREWORD
     Graham Cooke...13

PREFACE...15

PART 1

CHAPTER 1
     Created for Blessing...17

CHAPTER 2
     Downloading..33

CHAPTER 3
     Blessings in Disguise..43

CHAPTER 4
     Positioned for Blessing..61

PART 2

CHAPTER 5
     You Are Blessed with Favor..71

CHAPTER 6
     You Are Blessed with Victory...83

CHAPTER 7
    You Are Blessed with Abundance....................................93

CHAPTER 8
    You Are Blessed with Health and Strength.................109

CHAPTER 9
    You Are Blessed with Everlasting Love........................119

THE BENEDICTION...131

APPENDIX
    Prophetic Decree – Favor..137

    Scripture Meditations for Life in the Blessing Zone..........143

FOREWORD

I thoroughly enjoyed *In the Zone*. When I was reading the manuscript I used parts of it in my devotional times with the Lord. I found that I had to stop reading just to give thanks and rejoice. It pulls you into a place of intimate reflection. It gently pressures you to contemplate the magnitude of the love of God.

It is vital to have a radiant idea of God, because then you can understand God's radiant idea of yourself. When you have a radiant idea of the Kingdom, then you can get a radiant idea of church as a community of friends living a life full of love and laughter.

Patricia loves encounter, experiences and empowerment. Thankfully I have been her friend for years. She loves to be in the Presence of God. She is a worshipper with a strong sense of wonder. Her life is all about encountering the love of the Father, experiencing the permission in the fullness of Christ, and being empowered by the Holy Spirit. This book is fully aligned with who she has become in the Lord Jesus.

The Gospel is such incredible Good News; it's too good to be true! The world is a cynical place at times. In business, anyone will tell you, if a deal looks too good to be true, someone is about to be played for a sucker. The Kingdom has no edge, what you see in Christ is precisely what is available. The issue is that we must have a heart encounter with the Father so that we can receive it, and we need our mind renewed in Christ so that we can perceive the fullness of everything God has planned for us. Lastly we must have a deep relationship with the Holy Spirit so that we inhabit this place in the best possible manner.

We need do nothing to enter this place; it is a gift from the Father. He has taken us out of darkness and placed us into Christ, the Kingdom of Light. He put us into the one place where He could shower us with love and affection whilst He works on making us into His image. We are a work in progress, receiving all the benefits of fullness as we partake of the process.

We need do nothing to enter into Christ; we must do everything to stay in Him. Abiding is the key discipline of a life lived in the Spirit. To learn to be seated in Christ as an attitude of peaceful rest. To stand in Him as an act of war. To dwell in Him as a fact of life. *"In Him we live and move and have our being" [Acts 17:28]*.

This is a great book to teach us who we are and how to remain in Christ. Jesus makes everything tangible, religious people make it theoretical. Never trust a theology that is not rooted in encounter, experience and empowerment. Theology is not the theory of life in the spirit, but the practice.

This book is a powerful tool in enabling us to examine ourselves in the love of the Father. We examine ourselves so that we can see what He sees. In communion, we examine ourselves [Dokimazo = to look at with a view to approval...1 Corinthians 11:28] so that we can drink the cup and eat the bread.

We prove [peirazo = look for evidence to approve...2 Corinthians 13:5] and examine [dokimazo] who we are in Jesus at every opportunity. We look at the power of the Gospel with a view to seeing ourselves in the place of God's choosing so that we can upgrade our abiding. Favor is the intentional bias of the Father towards us in Christ. Your secret place is the personal space you have with God that provides you with ongoing encounters of His Presence, maintains and develops your current experiences of Jesus, and empowers you to abide in that life and release it to others.

It is the place where you have proved God and abide in His nature. "In the Zone" should never be too far from your bible. It is an excellent devotional and meditation tool. I loved the Decrees and Scripture Promises in Part Two; Decrees and Promises concerning Favor, Victory, Abundance, Health and Strength, and the Everlasting Love of the Father. Brilliant.

Our circumstances are not the problem. Our perceptions of our circumstances are often our biggest source of stress. In this book Patricia gives us astonishing keys to unlocking our insights on God's nature and permission. We must disempower our disappointments and empower our expectations.

Graham Cooke, *Friend of Patricia King*

PREFACE

What zone do **you** live in?

Did you know that Jesus carved out a realm of perpetual abundance and goodness for you through His finished work on the cross? This realm has your name on it! I call that realm **The Zone**. It is the Blessing Zone! You were created for blessing and blessed you shall be. You can live in this Zone of goodness, health, victory, peace, joy, and prosperity all the days of your life in the earth.

When you live in the Blessing Zone, you are blessed in everything you put your hands to. Your health is blessed. Your finances are blessed. Your family is blessed. Your workplace is blessed. Your relationships are blessed. Blessings come upon you and overtake you. Difficulties and challenges turn into blessings for you. Curses flee from you. Yes, this is life in The Zone. Would you enjoy living in such a realm of bliss? You can!

Many believers understand that when they finish their course of life in the earth, they will step into heaven where all is lovely, perfect, and awesome. This is true of course, but most do not understand that they can experience this inheritance now.

Would you be interested in such a life today? There are other zones you can choose if you want. There is the curse zone, the zone of mediocrity, the zone of lack, the zone of just enough and of course numerous others. The choice is yours.

Make a quality decision today that will determine the Zone you live in for the rest of your life. Step into The Blessing Zone. How? Read the following pages and allow the Holy Spirit to usher you in!

PART ONE

CHAPTER

1

CREATED FOR BLESSING

God blessed them; and God said to them,
"Be fruitful and multiply…" Genesis 1:28

UPGRADED

"Wake up! You are being upgraded!" My husband and I had just settled into our economy seats on the United Air flight to Hawaii in September 2008. We were drifting off to sleep when a voice of someone standing beside us announced these words, "You are being upgraded!" I opened my eyes to see a flight attendant, who repeated the announcement to us, "You are being upgraded. Come quickly."

We collected our carry-on items and followed the attendant to our newly assigned seats in Row 9. It was the most prestigious business class I had ever experienced! It seemed unusually large and featured all the latest "bells and whistles." We enjoyed all the luxuries of business class while feeling very surreal about the encounter.

The Holy Spirit spoke to me on various levels regarding this upgrade. He revealed the following interpretation for the body of Christ: "I am upgrading My people to business class – Father's business, that is. Not as servants but as sons and daughters. My children are seated in heavenly places in Christ far above all principalities, powers and dominions. They will soar far above all the conflicts and restraints in the earth. The Holy Spirit's gifts and fruit will manifest through My people in this hour. Both My character and My power will be established in these coming days."

ANOTHER UPGRADE

We arrived in Hawaii at 7:00 a.m., so we requested an early check-in at the hotel registration desk. "Why, of course, Mr. and Mrs. King. In fact, we have upgraded you to an *ocean view* with a king bed," the clerk informed. They then escorted us to *Room 2812*.

That year, the Lord had highlighted for me the book of Deuteronomy in which to receive special personal promises, especially the promises in Deuteronomy 28:12. "The LORD will open for you His good storehouse, the heavens, to give rain to your land in its season and to bless all the work of your hand; and you shall lend to many nations, but you shall not borrow."

On the very day we checked into our room, the stock market crashed to an all-time low. The television told the story of the shaking that was taking place in the world's economic system, but we were safe and secure in *Room 2812*.

The Lord spoke this word to me, "My promises are yes and amen for My children. The world and its systems will surely be shaken, but My children shall not be shaken when they find their shelter and refuge in Me. They will live in the safety of My blessings. They will live in *2812*. You must believe My Word. You must trust Me fully in this hour. My children shall live in My blessings and by My blessings."

While the world was being shaken around us, Ron and I were living more than comfortably in an upgraded room with an ocean view and king bed. We were surrounded by blessing. This is a true prophetic picture for all who walk upright in Him.

You are invited to live in the blessings of God – to live an upgraded life!

CREATED FOR BLESSING

You were created for blessing. That is why you desire the goodness of God to manifest in your life. It feels good and it feels right when you are blessed because you were made for it. After God created mankind He made a decree, "God blessed them..." Genesis 1:28a.

One of the definitions of *bless* in the Merriam Webster's Online Dictionary is, "to confer prosperity or happiness upon." Blessings speak of the goodness of God. Imagine for a moment your life being full of everything good all the time. That is God's desire for you. That is what it means to be blessed!

In Deuteronomy 28:2 we discover a promise that is so amazing, and yet it belongs to anyone who qualifies. It says, "All these blessings will come upon you and overtake you." The scenario that this Scripture reminds me of is that of a football game when a player gets aggressively tackled from behind and brought down. His opponent came upon him and overtook him. Imagine what it would be like if blessings came upon your life in that way. They can and they will when you determine to live in The Zone!

Deuteronomy 28:1 gives the terms of qualification and the instruction for posturing yourself to receive the blessings. "*If* you will diligently obey *all* the commandments…" (Emphasis mine). Oh no! What do we do now? How can we qualify? No one has ever obeyed *all* the Lord's commandments all the time… except for Jesus! The good news is this: because Jesus fulfilled all righteousness for you, He opened the way for you to live in all the promises, all the time. All the blessings listed in Deuteronomy 28:1-12 and in the rest of the Bible are yours not because of your own righteousness but because of His. They are not yours because you are worthy but because He is. He fulfilled the requirements and gave you the blessings – blessings that will come upon you and overtake you on a perpetual basis. This is truly a picture of what it means to "live in The Zone."

When my grandson was a baby, I played a game with him. I crawled on the floor behind him and said, "Grandma's going to get you!" He actually wanted me to get him. He would attempt to crawl away from me so that I could catch him. That was the fun part. He would laugh and then attempt to crawl away again, looking behind him to see if I was going to come and catch him up into my arms and kiss him all over. Of course, I got him every time. I came up from behind and overtook him with love hugs and kisses. At five years of age, he still enjoyed the "*Grandma's going to get you*" game, and his little sister picked up on it really well, too. This is a great picture of how blessings can come upon you and overtake you. They are looking for you. They want to catch you. They want to "get you." And of course, you want them to. Right?

ALL THE BLESSINGS ARE YOURS

Ephesians 1:3 says, "Blessed be the God and Father of our Lord Jesus Christ, who has blessed us with every spiritual blessing in the heavenly places in Christ." Through the finished work of the cross you have been blessed with every spiritual blessing. Jesus explains to us in John 17:22 that the glory the Father gave Him He has freely given to us. The word *glory (doxa)* in that context includes all the blessings of who God is and what He has. You are called to live in the abundance of these blessings. The Scripture calls them spiritual blessings in Christ. They are called spiritual because they are in the unseen or spiritual dimension. They are secured for you in the heavenly places in Christ where He is seated at the right hand of the Father. They are therefore safe from the influence of the demonic because they are in Christ. In another chapter, I will teach you how to exercise your faith in order to download all these blessings into your "now."

YOU HAVE EVERYTHING YOU NEED RIGHT NOW

You do not need to wait until the chariots come to take you away to the sweet by and by to receive a life of blessing. This is your portion NOW due to Christ's finished work of the cross. Peter wrote, "His divine power has granted to us everything pertaining to life and godliness, through the true knowledge of Him who called us by His own glory and excellence. For by these He has granted to us His precious and magnificent promises, so that by them you may become partakers of the divine nature, having escaped the corruption that is in the world by lust" (2 Peter 1:3-4).

Let's break this passage into segments and meditate on the glorious promises contained therein. Receive all the Lord is giving to you in this portion of Scripture.

...His divine power has granted to us...

There are two important things to note in this verse. First, that it is not your own power or striving that obtains the blessings, but it is God Himself who has prepared the table for you.

Secondly, it is to be noted that the blessings have already been given. "Granted" is past tense. You do not have to hope that God will possibly grant you some blessings today or tomorrow. They have already been given. When were they given to you? At the cross!

Two thousand years ago an eternal, unbreakable covenant was cut between God and man. A covenant is a legally binding agreement between two individuals or between two parties of people. In order for a covenant to remain valid, both parties must keep all the terms of the covenant all the time. God fulfilled all His terms for this covenant and then He became man and fulfilled all of man's terms. It is a done deal. The One who created the covenant has also fulfilled the covenant and He will keep it for all eternity. Jesus is your representative in this covenant. He fulfilled all the law and all the prophecies and ever lives to stand in the gap for you. This covenant includes the establishing of all the blessings and the dissolving of all the curses. You cannot wreck, ruin, or destroy this covenant because you did not make it. He did. He has given the rights of this covenant to everyone who believes in Him.

You enter this amazing covenant the moment you invite Jesus into your heart as your personal Lord and Savior and receive forgiveness of sins. You become one with Jesus and He becomes one with you when you invite Him to come into your heart. Entering into Christ and Christ entering into you grants you full access all the time into this awesome covenant that God prepared on your behalf. If you have never invited Christ into your life, now is a great time. He is a blessing God. He is pure Love and He desires to give you new life right now. If you sincerely desire to start a new life, a blessed life with Jesus as your Savior and Lord, simply pray the following prayer with sincere faith and He will come into your heart immediately. You will then be His child. Your name will be written in the book of life in heaven. He will be your God.

Dear Heavenly Father, I believe that Jesus Christ died on the cross for my sins. I invite Christ to come into my heart right now and forgive me of all my sin and fill me with new life. I invite Christ to be my personal Savior and Lord. I receive this new and blessed life by faith. Thank You, Father, for the great loving kindness You have shown me. Thank You for the new life I now have in Jesus. AMEN

If you just prayed that prayer, then welcome to the family of God! Your name is written in His book of life in heaven. You are God's own child – forever!

...Everything pertaining to life and godliness...

I like to emphasize the *"everything"* in this verse. How much is everything? It truly is *every* thing! This promise is amazing. Everything that you need to live an abundant life is yours right now. It is available to you. It has your name on it! And there is more. Peter goes on to say that everything that pertains to *godliness* is yours now, too. You don't have to strive to be godly. You don't have to beat yourself up. You do not need to faint as a result of grueling, self-effort. You have been given by God's own will and power everything that pertains to godliness. Your righteousness, strength, health, prosperity, wisdom and peace are all yours in Christ. You have all these things *now*. They are yours.

...Through the true knowledge of Him who called us by His own glory and excellence...

You will receive the manifest blessings as you grow in the knowledge of Him. All life is wrapped up in Jesus Christ and without Him you have no true life at all. The "knowledge" this verse is referring to is revelation knowledge – the knowledge that comes by the Holy Spirit. The Holy Spirit has been given to you by your Father in heaven to reveal Christ and the mysteries of the Kingdom of God. The Holy Spirit will disclose to you that which is yours in Jesus. Jesus said, "He (referring to the Holy Spirit) will glorify Me, for He will take of Mine and will disclose it to you. All things that the Father has are Mine; therefore I said that He takes of Mine and will disclose it to you" (John 16:14,15).

This is absolutely amazing but true – the Father gave all things to the Son and in Him has freely given them to you (John 3:35). Then He gave you the Holy Spirit to show you what has been given. He discloses to you what is yours in Christ through revelation. Whatever He reveals is yours to embrace and to live in to the fullest.

...He has granted to us His precious and magnificent promises...

Look carefully, because Peter again emphasizes that these things have already been given. They have been granted. Not *going to be* but *have been*. What has been given? The precious and magnificent promises. All the blessings (precious and magnificent blessings) have been given to you already. If you can find a precious and magnificent promise in the Word, it is yours!

...So that by them you may become partakers of the divine nature...

This is awesome! God desires you to partake of His divine nature by living according to the promises. When you live in the blessings of God, you partake of His nature. He is a blessing God. His Kingdom is full of goodness and light and there is no darkness in Him at all. When you live in the blessings it is like heaven on earth. You become like Christ when you live in the Blessing Zone. The atmosphere of heaven envelops you.

...Having escaped the corruption that is in the world by lust...

Lust finds its power when a soul feels unfulfilled. When you know beyond a shadow of a doubt that the Lord Himself will fulfill every need and that He has already given you everything that pertains to fullness of life, then you escape the temptations that are in the world. Focusing on the blessings and receiving them by faith actually can deliver you from lust. Jesus is your ultimate fulfillment for everything pertaining to life.

LIFE IN THE KINGDOM

In the invisible realm there are two Kingdoms. One is a Kingdom of blessing and life and the other a Kingdom of curse and death. You get to choose which Kingdom you live in.

A Kingdom is a territory where a king has rule. It is the domain or the jurisdiction of a king. In the invisible realm there is the Kingdom of God and the Kingdom of Satan. You belong to one or the other depending on who has rule over your life. There is no neutral ground. God's Kingdom is a Kingdom of love, honor, goodness, purity, blessing and abundance. Satan's Kingdom is full of hate, strife, confusion, darkness, curse, and destruction. When you look at what each Kingdom has to offer, there is actually only one choice that makes any sense at all. You don't have to be a rocket scientist to figure it out. God is good and the devil is bad. Following God brings goodness into your life and not following Him leaves you with the devil's consequences.

To live in the Kingdom of God, you submit to the King and follow His laws just like in a natural kingdom. The Bible has been given to you so you will have a handbook for Kingdom life. I love the Bible! It is a book of life, wisdom, love and blessing. It contains truth, and the truth blesses you with great freedom and liberty. When you live by the Bible's instruction, you are truly blessed in all things.

THE FATHER HAS CHOSEN TO GIVE YOU HIS KINGDOM

Jesus said, "Do not be afraid, little flock, for your Father has chosen gladly to give you the kingdom" (Luke 12:32). This is outrageous! Your Heavenly Father delights in giving you the Kingdom. What does that look like? Jesus taught you to pray in this way, "Your Kingdom come. Your will be done, on earth as it is in heaven" (Matthew 6:10). He would not have taught you to pray that way if He didn't want you to have the download of heaven's blessings in your life now.

Take some time to dream for a few moments. What would your life look like if you lived in the atmosphere of God's Kingdom? Can you imagine the abundance you would live in? The peace? The rest? The love? The creativity? I love dreaming like this and what makes it truly enjoyable is to understand that God delights in freely giving all these things to us. He has chosen gladly to give you His Kingdom – the full domain of King Jesus. It is almost incomprehensible, yet absolutely true. Why would you want to live anywhere else other than under the rule of King Jesus, the King of Love, the King of Blessing?

HERE COMES THE QUEEN

One of my favorite stories in the Bible is when the Queen of Sheba visited King Solomon (see 1 Kings 10). King Solomon was living in the extravagant blessings of God and the testimony of this spread to the nations around him. He was blessed with wisdom beyond measure and with wealth that was greater than any other.

There was so much blessing in Solomon's life that the Queen of Sheba did not believe the reports that she had heard. As a result, she went to visit Solomon. She tested him with difficult questions and he answered every one with the magnificent wisdom that God had granted him. Then Solomon took her on a tour of his estate. She was so overwhelmed with the blessings of Solomon's house that she actually fainted! It all took her breath away.

This is a picture of what the Lord is calling you to. You, like Solomon, are called to live in the glory of your King's Kingdom. It is all yours! In Christ you have been made a king and priest unto Him (Revelation 1:6).

The glory the Father gave Jesus has been given to you (John 17:22). You, like Solomon, can cause the nations to be drawn to the brightness of your rising. Isaiah 60 describes this. There will be a people that will arise in the glory (blessings) that will literally attract the attention of kings, nations, and wealth.

You might think, "But Solomon was a special king and was set into place by his father King David." You might argue, "But God especially visited Solomon in a dream and offered him his desire. God blessed Solomon with wisdom and wealth in a unique way." Really? Do you realize that you are very much like Solomon? Think of this. First of all, you have been set into place as a king by your Heavenly King, just like Solomon was by his earthly king (father). Revelation 1:6 states that Jesus, "...hath made us *kings* and priests unto God" (KJV). Solomon was invited by God to ask Him for anything and it would be given. You have the same in Jesus. "If you ask Me anything in My name, I will do it" (John 14:14).

In the dream Solomon received from the Lord, he asked God for wisdom. God was impressed with him that he asked for wisdom. As a result God gave Him riches also. Why? Because "wisdom *is* the principal thing; therefore get wisdom. And in all your getting, get understanding" (Proverbs 4:7 NKJV). When you have wisdom, you also have riches, honor and long life. "Long life is in her *(wisdom's)* right hand; in her left hand are riches and honor" (Proverbs 3:16). Solomon had both wisdom and riches because riches are in wisdom. He asked for the principal thing and got everything a king could desire and need.

When the Queen of Sheba saw his wisdom and his riches, she was amazed to the point of "fainting." I personally believe she fell under the power of the Spirit due to the weight of the glory in Solomon's house. This also took place with the priests when Solomon dedicated the temple. In one accord they declared, "The Lord is good and His mercy endures forever." As they declared His goodness, the glory filled the house and they fell under the power. I believe that this is exactly what happened to the Queen of Sheba. She saw the glory and fell under the power of the Spirit. She then proclaimed, "You exceed in wisdom and prosperity the report which I heard" (1 Kings 10:7).

Due to the visible display of blessing in Solomon's life, the heathen queen became a worshipper of the true and living God. I love this! She declared, "Blessed be the LORD your God who delighted in you to set you on the throne of Israel…therefore He made you king, to do justice and right-eousness" (1 Kings 10:9). YES! This is what being blessed is all about! Solomon was made King so that he could establish righteousness and justice.

God so desires His people to be blessed with His glorious goodness. In Isaiah 60, the prophet declares that during a time of great darkness that will cover the earth and its people, the Lord will raise up His children to shine and manifest His glory. The word "glory" refers to the fullness of all God is and has, but in the context of this chapter specifically refers to riches and abundance. The prophet declares how even kings and nations will come as the glory (riches and abundance) appears upon us. He describes how they will come forth with wealth, camels, gold, silver, bronze, iron and frankincense. We see this happening in the life of Solomon. The Queen of Sheba came with camels, gold, silver, gems, spices and other things when she heard about the glory of Solomon's life and house.

This level of blessing has a purpose: the execution of righteousness and justice in the earth. This is what the Queen of Sheba understood when she saw the bounty. It wasn't about Solomon's personal wealth, it was about what he did with it. That is why she praised the Lord for making him king, so that he would establish justice and righteousness. Beloved, this is what we are called to today. God is going to bless us so that we can be a blessing!

For years we have been sowing into the needs of the orphans and the poor. Recently we have been helping to rescue child soldiers and lives that have been trapped in the sex trade. It is not just or righteous for anyone to be exploited in such ways. One day I was dreaming before the Lord and thought, "If we had multiple millions of dollars we could build orphanages and homes for the children at risk and also build micro-businesses for girls coming out of the sex trade." I continued to dream big and envisioned what it would be like if billions of dollars came into the hands of the church. We already had the privilege of helping to build a few orphanages, but I had this desire to go after greater wealth. I asked the Lord for $100,000 to build an orphanage to rescue child soldiers. I locked into this by faith, declaring the blessing zone around my heart's desire. It amazed me that in less than a month of the desire coming into my heart, the full need was met! In a two day period, God enabled me to raise the funds for the orphanage. Now we are building more – and we will continue to build more and more and more.

The blessing zone is full of multiplication. This is what it looks like to execute righteousness and justice in the earth. If all of us received the blessings in order to be a blessing then the world would truly be transformed.

We have discovered that whenever we reach out to sow into the lives and needs of the poor, we get blessed back enormously in return. You can never outgive God. When we build houses for the poor, the Lord blesses us with increase in our own lives and often with land, home, and building ownership. We don't even look for it – it just comes. Blessings come upon us and overtake us. We can't help it. This is what it is like to live in the Zone.

Some people believe that if you have the world's goods, you have to give them all away and leave nothing for yourself if you are going to be truly spiritual. This is not true. When you give everything away, then you have resource in your heavenly account that you can draw from (and the interest rate in heaven is a *wowzer* – 30-60-100- and even 1000-fold increase.) I have tried to outgive the Lord at times and I cannot. The more I give to Him, the more He gives back!

Jesus invited the rich young ruler to give everything he had to the poor and promised him that he would have treasure in heaven (Matthew 19:21). This is such a key! Jesus did not instruct him to give everything away and be poor. He made it clear that if he sowed everything, he would have treasure to draw from in his heavenly account. The rich young ruler could not do it because he loved his riches in the world more than heavenly economy. He lacked faith and trust in the Kingdom of God.

When the Queen of Sheba saw the goodness of God demonstrated in Solomon's life, she then endowed Solomon with many more blessings. Blessings attract blessings. Solomon was blessed with great wisdom, wealth and honor. He was blessed beyond measure so that he could be a blessing.

Yes, he enjoyed life in The Zone. So can you!

God is raising up a company of believers in this hour who live in the blessing realm. This company will be so incredibly blessed that they will cause those who do not know the Lord to be shocked and in awe of the splendor and majesty of His Kingdom. These believers will be overtaken by blessings. They will be blessed in everything they put their hands to. They will be blessed as they rise up in the morning and blessed when they sleep at night. All their relationships will be blessed. Their finances will be blessed. Their health will be blessed. They will increase in houses, lands, and vehicles. They will be fruitful and multiply. They will be blessed with great favor. They will shine as lights in the darkest of places. Their darkness will shine like the noonday (Isaiah 58:10). Goodness and mercy shall follow them all the days of their lives (Psalm 23:6).

What a company! This is truly glorious! What about you? Do you desire to be in that company? Do you want to live in The Zone? Then go for it! You have been granted free access through Christ. You really have!

2

DOWNLOADING

*"Without faith it is impossible to please Him, for he who
comes to God must believe that He is and that
He is a rewarder of those who seek Him."*
Hebrews 11:6

Abraham is well known for his faith and for being a son of blessing. Before Abraham was visited by God, he and his family were Chaldean moon worshippers. The Lord invited him to leave his family, beliefs, and the land of his residence to follow Him. Abraham did not know where the Lord would lead him, but he did have a revelation of His goodness, and he believed. He trusted God's goodness and left everything to follow Him, not knowing where he was going. The Lord was deeply touched by Abraham's faith and obedience. As a result, all the nations to this day are invited to enter the blessing of eternal life prepared in Christ (Abraham's offspring). Because Abraham believed, he entered a covenant of blessing with God. That covenant of blessing was fulfilled for all of us in Christ and remains to this day for all who believe.

Genesis 12:2 says, "And I will make you a great nation, and I will bless you, and make your name great; and so you shall be a blessing."

Abraham entered into the covenant of blessing through faith, but he had to walk it out when it did not look like blessing was manifesting. The Lord confirmed His promise to Abraham at ninety-nine years of age that he would be a father of many nations (Genesis 17:6). He then sent "messengers" to both Abraham and Sarah to declare that they would have a son within the year (Genesis 18:1-19). It is remarkable that he received this promise, since he was past the time in the natural when he could produce children.

"In hope against hope he believed, so that he might become a father of many nations according to that which had been spoken, 'so shall your descendants be' " (Romans 4:18).

Abraham's faith saw the promise when there was nothing in the natural realm that he could possibly see. He saw with Kingdom vision. His faith in the promise of God caused him to live in the blessing and reality of fruitfulness even before the promise manifest. Abraham is the Father of unshakable faith.

Through faith, the promise God gave him became his internal reality. He is a great example for the church today. The example of his faith is an important key to life in The Zone.

THE FAITH CONNECTION

As we have discovered, all the blessings are already yours in Christ. Everything that pertains to life and godliness has already been given to you through Christ's death on the cross. The Word makes it clear that the promises are yours. You simply need the faith connection activated to bring the promises out of the invisible Kingdom realm into manifestation in your life. If you do not understand how to "download" with your faith, then even though all the promises are available to you, they will not benefit you. You must appropriate the promises through faith.

ENJOY THE BUFFET

I often think of a buffet scenario to explain this. I love food! As a result I find buffets extremely enjoyable. After you purchase your ticket for the buffet you can eat as much as you want and whatever you want. When you enter a buffet, you go through the entrance with your ticket and are usually seated at a table by a hostess.

Imagine an individual sitting down at the table and then screaming out to the waitress, "I'm hungry!!!! I'm so hungry." In shock, the hostess replies, "Well, dear one, go and get some food. We have salads, meat dishes, breads and spreads, vegetables, and dessert." The customer responds by saying, "Oh that sounds very good, but I am so hungry, if only I had something to eat. It all looks so good!" Perplexed, the hostess again replies, "Ma'am, please go and get something to eat. It has been prepared for you." The customer continues to whine about how hungry she is, but doesn't go to fill her plate with what had already been purchased. She is in a buffet, but she could possibly starve even though there is food all around her. The food had been prepared and beautifully set out for her, but she did not realize that she had to fill her plate.

In the same way, many Christians starve in the realm of promises and blessings. Christ paid the price of the "ticket" for you to enter into blessings and eternal life two thousand years ago. His Kingdom is full of blessings for you! You have entered the banquet feast of blessings through Christ's finished work on the cross. You simply need to fill your plate (life) with His goodness. He has prepared everything. He has set it out for you. It is now time to receive the blessings.

Many are like the woman who said she was so hungry even though there was food all around her. They have identified the hunger but have not identified the blessings that are already theirs. They look at the promises from afar but don't realize they have access. All the woman needed to do was go and fill her plate. Your faith is what fills your life (plate) full of blessings. The promises are set before you, and your faith secures them.

STALE CRACKERS AND MOLDY CHEESE

I was once told a story about a man in Europe who wanted to travel to America. He had very limited funds but worked hard saving every extra penny he could in order to purchase a ticket on a liner. He found a very good rate and bought the least expensive ticket, which gave him very humble quarters shared with others in the bottom of the ship. He prepared for the 20-day voyage by packing a few items of clothing and a 20-day supply of crackers and cheese as he had no extra funds for meals.

During mealtimes his bunkmates invited him to join them but he insisted that he would stay in his room. He had rationed his portions of crackers and cheese out perfectly so he would have food to last for the 20-day journey. By the fifteenth day, the crackers became very stale and the cheese grew mold and could not be eaten. As a result, he fasted the rest of the journey. He would lie in his bed during the mealtime and feel sorry for himself. He was hungry.

The ship finally landed on American shores. As he was in the line to disembark the ship, one of the crew members said to him, "We've been on this ship for 20 days, but I have not seen you at one meal. Where were you?" He answered, "Well to be honest with you, I could only afford the least expensive ticket, and I did not have any extra for food, so I stayed in my room during the meals. The crew member looked shocked and said, "Didn't you realize that the meals were included in the ticket?"

Oh, my gosh! All he had to do was go and fill his plate. Every meal was included in the price of the ticket. Jesus paid the price for our ticket and it is an all-inclusive package.

Faith is Substance

"Faith is the substance of things hoped for, the evidence of things not seen" (Hebrews 11:1 NKJV). Faith is an actual spiritual substance and it is very powerful, as it is the force that brings those things out of the invisible realm into manifestation! It is the substance of what you hope for. Hope is not wishful thinking but rather a joyful expectation. The woman mentioned in the buffet scenario was whining over her need. She was hungry and she wanted to be filled. She cried out with her need and desire, but God does not respond to need, He responds to faith. A need doesn't constitute a miracle, faith does. Faith needs true hope (not whining) in order to be birthed, for it is the substance of things hoped for.

Let's look at another example. A man looks at his desk and there are five unpaid bills that amount to $5,000. He then looks at his bank account and discovers that he is overdrawn by $500. He is shocked and initially without hope. He is overwhelmed. He cries out, "Oh God, I am in a mess. I have a stack of bills and an empty bank account. Oh God, help me. What am I going to do? I sure *hope* they will get paid." He then falls on his face and weeps and wails. This is not actually hope yet. He is definitely sharing the devastation of his heart and the details of the problem, but he is not in hope.

Hope would look like this: "Wow! Look at this. My bills are enormous and I have no money in the bank. I can hardly wait to see how the Lord is going to lead me to overcome." He then worships and praises the Lord, because he has hope. He has joyful expectation for the Lord's promises and goodness to be made manifest.

Faith is the substance of what you hope for, not what you whine for. When you are in faith, you have moved from joyful expectation (hope) to a strong unshakable belief that is your internal reality. Faith seals what you hope for. You no longer look for what you hope for, you already have it. You are 100% confident within that it is a done deal. It is your internal reality.

Faith is the evidence of what is not yet visible to your natural vision. Abraham believed the promise that he would be the father of many nations even when his natural abilities to produce the manifestation of the promise were no longer an option. His faith in God's Word was the evidence of what he could not see in the natural. It was his internal reality. He was unshakable in his faith and his faith impressed God greatly. He chose to believe God's Word rather than his circumstance. Faith grows through your choice to believe.

Hebrews 11:6 says, "Without faith it is impossible please Him…" With faith, you certainly can – just like Abraham did. To live in the blessing zone you must exercise your "downloader"– your faith. The promises are all invisible, but your faith makes them evident. Faith is the evidence of things not seen. The promises of God will give you hope until your faith makes them substance. Faith is the substance of things hoped for. All the promises are in the invisible realm of the Kingdom of God. They are eternal realities that need to become your internal realities through the operation of your faith. The promises download out of the heavenly places in Christ into your life through faith. Faith is the connector. Faith is the downloader. When they are downloaded by faith, then they are yours. After the promise is secured by faith then you will experience the manifestation in the natural realm.

Jesus said, "All things are possible to him who believes" (Mark 9:23). Faith is the downloader for all things that are possible in Jesus. This is both amazing and extremely exciting!

RECEIVE FAITH

The Bible tells us that we are all given "a measure of faith" (Romans 12:3). Genesis 1:27 says, "God created man in His own image..." He is a faith God, so therefore we are faith people. Hebrews 11:3 says, "Through faith we understand that the worlds were framed by the word of God, so that things which are seen were not made of things which do appear" (KJV).

Through faith, God built the framework for the worlds through His declared Word. Everything that is seen in our natural vision came forth from an invisible realm through God's faith and decree. He has designed us to function in the same way. There are things invisible to you now.

"Faith comes from hearing, and hearing by the word of Christ" (Romans 10:17). The word *hearing* in this passage is referring to the *rhema* word or the word that is quickened to us by the Holy Spirit. Faith comes from the revealed word of God.

Deuteronomy 29:29 declares, "The secret things belong to the Lord our God, but the things revealed belong to us and to our sons forever..." When God reveals promises to you, the revealed word creates the faith in your heart to establish the blessing in your life. Faith comes by receiving the revealed, Spirit-inspired Word. I love Deuteronomy 29:29. It is actually saying that if you see it you can have it! When the Lord quickens a promise to you, He intends for that promise to be made manifest in your life. He does not reveal the promise to you so that you can merely think in your mind, "Oh, isn't that a nice promise?" No, the promises He quickens are true Kingdom realities and He wants them to tangibly manifest in your life.

Faith comes from hearing the revealed word of God. Therefore, it is vital that you posture yourself to receive the promises from Him. Mary of Bethany sat at the feet of Jesus and received His Word. She was postured to hear revelation that would create faith (see Luke 10:39).

Remember, "Faith comes from hearing and hearing by the Word of Christ." Normally, you cannot see Jesus with your natural vision, but He is always with you. He is invisible yet very real. Hebrews 11:6 says, "for he who comes to God must believe that He is and that He is a rewarder of those who seek Him." Believe He is with you. Take time to sit at His feet to hear His Word.

Search the Scriptures and invite the Holy Spirit to quicken promises of blessings to you. As soon as they are quickened, they are yours. Download them into your heart and establish them there. The excitement and joyful anticipation you feel when a promise is quickened is called hope. And hope produces faith.

FAITH – THE EVIDENCE

Faith is the substance of what you hope for, but it is also the evidence of what you cannot see (Hebrews 11:1). When my husband Ron and I were first born-again in 1976, we shared our experience with his father. It did not go over well at all. Ron's dad was upset and would say over and over again, "I am going to hell when I die and have a party with my friends." When we shared the gospel with him he would always get upset and angry. I was not moved by his reactions at all because I knew that he was saved even though we could not see the evidence of his salvation. We saw through the eyes of faith. I had read the Scriptures that birthed this faith. Acts 16:31 said, "Believe in the Lord Jesus, and you will be saved, you and your household." Psalm 2:8 stated, "Ask of me, and I shall give thee the heathen for thine inheritance" (KJV). 1 John 5:14,15 confirmed that if I prayed according to His will (and He wills that none would perish) that I would have whatever I asked.

These Scriptures were not just print on a page to me, they were internal realities. Even though I had not heard my father-in-law confess faith in Christ yet, he was already saved. Our faith was the evidence of what we could not see. God's Word said it and so it settled it for us. Twenty-seven years later he confessed his salvation but, for me, he was already secure in Christ. My faith said so. It was reality. It was evidence.

Faith is the substance of what you hope for and it is the evidence of what you cannot see. The more you meditate on the promises, the more your hope will establish faith. Before you know it, the promises will be unshakable Kingdom reality within you. This reality is called faith. When it is established substance within you, then it will manifest within the realm of time. It is like a baby. I remember when my son and daughter-in-law were expecting our first grandchild. The moment he was conceived, he was a living being. We could not see him yet, but he was an internal reality for sure. He continued to grow in the womb and eventually he was born into visibility where we could hold him, touch him, and look at all his features. He had to be an internal reality first, and then in the fullness of time he was manifest in our arms. The entire time he was hidden in the womb, we said, "We have a grandchild," because we did!

This is a picture of your faith. Faith is internal reality that is based on the promises of God. By faith, you can download into your soul all the blessings that are revealed to you. When the Holy Spirit reveals it, you believe and receive it. It is yours in the womb of your soul through faith, and then eventually you will see it manifest. Become pregnant with blessings. All the promises of God are yours.

You can begin to live in the blessing zone right now. Determine today to live in the blessings of God – for the rest of your life. Make the quality decision – now… then get ready to download!

CHAPTER
3

BLESSINGS IN DISGUISE

And we know that God causes all things to work together for good to those who love God, to those who are called according to His purpose.
Romans 8:28

Oftentimes we miss discerning valuable blessings that come our way because they don't actually look or feel like blessings. I call them *blessings in disguise*.

When you live in The Zone, it is very important to strongly determine your blessing perimeters. This means you determine that nothing but blessings are given access into your life.

But what about things that come your way that don't look at all like blessings? What about the things you have no control over which certainly do not appear good?

Jesus taught us to pray for the Kingdom to come and for God's will to be done on earth as it is in heaven (see Matthew 6:10). We know that there is nothing evil in heaven. There is no sickness, disease, accident, lack, poverty, uncleanness, or sin of any kind. God's desire for us is to become established in Kingdom life and goodness all the time. You will experience only blessing in heaven and it is clear that this is what you are to pray for, to experience here and now. Heaven's standard is your standard. Paul taught you to "keep seeking the things above, where Christ is, seated at the right hand of God. Set your mind on the things above, not on the things that are on earth" (Colossians 3:1, 2). The kingdom of heaven is clearly your plumb line.

You are in the world, yet not of the world when you are in Christ (see John 17:16, 18). You are God's child and your citizenship is in heaven. Although you might understand that you are called to goodness, Jesus promised you that during your time in the world you will face tribulation. "In the world, you will have tribulation, but be of good cheer, I have overcome the world" (John 16:33 NKJV). So how can you expect to live a life free from the pressures in the world if Jesus promised you that you would definitely have tribulation? And furthermore, if you are to receive ONLY blessing, then how does this all fit? Tribulation doesn't appear to be a blessing. There is no tribulation in heaven.

IN THE WORLD – NOT OF THE WORLD

One of the greatest keys for you in this passage is that Jesus said to be of good cheer because He has already overcome the world. And you are in Him! The *world* refers to the systems of this age including its governments, economics, and values. This world system will definitely oppose the kingdom of heaven that lives in you, the one you dwell in by faith. The world is subject to the consequences of sin and as a result there is great turmoil in the world around you.

You, however, are not of the world but you are heavenly. You are in the world as a citizen of heaven but you are not *of* the world. You do not belong to it. Jesus said that we are to be of good cheer, because He has overcome the world. As you live in the world you will face tribulation. Jesus said so. You are not to let the tribulation knock you down and overcome you but rather you are to be of good cheer and overcome in Christ. When you overcome tribulation, you receive the blessing of the overcomer. Tribulation then becomes a blessing in disguise for you.

It is never over until it's over! And it is not over until you win. If you embrace this perspective then you will always triumph in Christ and the tribulation in the world that attempts to take you out will actually become the catalyst to your next promotion in Christ and in life.

Untouched by the Surrounding Darkness

In the book of Exodus we find Egypt pressuring and oppressing God's people. Even though their forefathers had aligned themselves with God, the Hebrews eventually forgot Him and began to worship the Egyptian gods instead. As a result, they continued to submit to the oppression of the world system for 400 years. They did not actually have to. Even in the Old Testament, God forgave when there was true repentance and contrition. He has always been a merciful God who pardons iniquity and He always will be. If God's people had only aligned with Him through a sincere, repentant heart, they would have escaped from living under the Egyptian "world system."

God in His goodness heard the cries of despair from His people and answered by raising up a deliverer named Moses. During the process of delivering His people out of Egypt, God executed judgments against the Egyptians. One of the judgments was darkness that filled the entire land. There was no light in any of the Egyptian homes. Nowhere was light found in Egypt… except in the homes of the Hebrews (Exodus 10:21-23). Their homes were filled with light. This is a great picture of how we can live with the darkness of the world all around us and yet we stand in The Zone of blessing that is untouched by the darkness.

The Choice

We choose whom we serve. If we choose God and His kingdom then we need to obey Him and His ways. If we submit to sin then we become the slave of sin (see Romans 6:16). God's people who were enslaved for 400 years in Egypt could have easily lived in the blessings of God if they had understood how to align with God. If they had repented, God would have forgiven and established them for all that time in His goodness. You can't serve two masters. You must choose whom you will serve.

Joseph lived in God's blessings even while in prison and became a great influence in Egypt during trying times. He aligned with God's ways and

Word and lived in the blessing zone as a result. It didn't matter if he was in the pit, Potiphar's house, the dungeon or the prison – he was blessed in the midst of the mistreatment and trials.

Daniel, in the midst of Babylon, lived in the favor and blessing of God. Babylon was the most brutal heathen nation in the earth at that time, and yet Daniel did not submit to the Babylonian world system. His people were enslaved and oppressed in Babylon, but Daniel did not live under oppression. He lived in the blessing zone. He was the head and not the tail, above and not beneath. He separated himself from the Babylonian world system even though he was in it. As a result he lived in enormous blessing. Even when the Babylonians attempted to kill him, he received testimonies of God's blessings that we are still in awe over to this day. He actually in some ways had more authority than the king because he influenced the King. Daniel was in Babylon, but not of it, and he was blessed. He lived in The Zone!

EVERYTHING WORKS TOGETHER FOR GOOD

When you are committed to living in The Zone, then you have assurance that everything that comes your way is unto blessing. "And we know that God causes all things to work together for good to those who love God, to those who are called according to His purpose" (Romans 8:28).

God has offered you breakthrough testimonies in everything that attempts to assault you. There is a reward of blessing within every trial. You simply have to secure it with your faith. The bigger the problem – the bigger the testimony. The greater the trial – the greater the reward. Tribulation in life turns into a blessing machine for those who determine to use it as a stepping-stone to greater levels and degrees of blessing in Christ. If you determine your blessing zone and by faith accept only blessings to come out of every situation, then everything adverse will indeed turn to good for you. You are the victor in Christ. You are the head and not the tail. You are above and not beneath.

RETURN TO SENDER

In my devotionals many years ago, the Lord gave me this funny scenario: A postman came to the door with a package. The package had my name on it. The sender's name was LU C FER. The content sticker said TROUBLE. The postman wanted me to sign for the package and receive it from him into my home. I thought, "Now, why would I want to sign for such a package?" I took the package and wrote RETURN TO SENDER and then closed the door.

The Lord was teaching me that it was my choice to receive blessing or curse. I decide whether or not to sign for the package. I determine what I allow into my life.

FINANCIAL CHALLENGES

Many years ago my husband Ron and I were called to leave our secular employment positions to pursue our evangelism call. We were given invitation by the Lord to live by raw faith with no visible means of support. We were very excited for the opportunity and after weighing up the Word and receiving numerous confirmations, we left our comfortable and lucrative places of employment to engage in this faith adventure.

The Lord put it on our hearts to go ONLY to Him with our material requests. We were not to tell anyone of our needs or accept any assistance from the government. We were in total agreement with this and full of faith and expectation when He proposed it to our hearts. We had studied all the Scriptures of God's supernatural intervention in the area of finance, and we had heard numerous testimonies of His faithfulness in the area of provisional miracles. We could hardly wait to encounter that miracle dimension. God was our only means of support as we launched into this faith adventure. We were not dependent on anyone or anything else – that is, once our savings account ran out.

The first few months were truly exciting and full of adventure as we believed God for supernatural provision. We saw miracles of provision manifest in many ways and, when we needed to, we fell back on our savings. In time, our savings were fully depleted, and then we were truly left without any options or exceptions. God alone had to come through or we were in deep trouble! For a five-year period, spirits of lack, poverty, and degradation assaulted us daily. They knocked on the door of our hearts continuously. We had to choose if we were going to sign for their packages or not.

We praised the Lord with all our hearts when our needs were visibly met, but would we praise Him when it appeared that the well had run dry? Would we still believe His promises and trust Him when the fridge was empty and when there was no available means to pay bills? Would we still find praise within our hearts to offer to Him when our hearts were broken and fearful? Would we still believe?

We had fully committed ourselves to the Lord's invitation to live by faith with sincerity and abandonment when we began this journey. We lined up our confirmations and obtained the blessing and agreement of our spiritual leaders. We studied the Scriptures from Genesis through Revelation and discovered that the Lord's promises were sure regarding provision. Nowhere did He say that He would not meet our needs. We also studied kingdom economy and believed and obeyed the wisdom and instruction of the Word regarding tithing, sowing and reaping, diligence, work ethics, and wise stewardship. We were fully committed to aligning with Him and His glorious Kingdom ways.

We struggled daily due to the enormous pressures that were against us. We had two young children who were such troopers during this time. They never complained or put any pressure on us. They embraced the faith walk also, and they always had praise in their hearts for God even though the days were extremely lean. There were times when our fridge was empty and we had no food. We literally had to pray for our daily bread. We served the Lord diligently with all our hearts and stood on the promises every day without wavering. In the midst of our faith struggles, we were scorned by family members and friends who did not understand our walk. Shame attempted to cloak us.

In the wrestling, we would always go back to God's sure Word and promises. We did not have a Plan B. We had all our eggs in one basket and were determined to stand in faith and not compromise. We found praise in our hearts for the goodness of God every day, and most days that praise was a true sacrifice.

When the postman attempted to deliver LU C FER's packages of shame, lack and poverty, we refused to sign for them. We closed the door on those options and decreed again the sure promises of God. Every day it was a trial and every day we had to choose God and His blessings over the lies of the enemy. We had to set our blessing perimeters.

I wish I could tell you that I passed every faith test perfectly during that time, but I did not. There were times when I screamed at God saying, *"Where are you? Even the heathen are blessed more than us and we are serving You with all our hearts!"*

I want to be open and vulnerable with you on this. I failed many times when the pressure became great. The good news is that when I confessed my sin and failure before God, He forgave me and cleansed me from all unrighteousness. My failures have been dissolved in the precious blood of Christ. I am sharing my failures with you so that you can be encouraged, but in God's eyes I passed the tests perfectly. He sees only my walk of faith. He does not see my failure. He cast my shortcomings and sinful responses of fear, unbelief and doubt, far from Him – as far as the east is from the west. They are remembered no more! They are gone! How awesome is He? Oh, how I love Him!

The five years of progressive attack and assault on our faith actually strengthened our faith even though it felt like we were being weakened. That is why the Word says, "Let the weak say, I am strong" (Joel 3:10 KJV). We overcame by standing on the covenant Word of God and testifying of His goodness. "They overcame him by the blood of the Lamb, and by the word of their testimony; and they loved not their lives unto the death" (Revelation 12:11 KJV).

One day in the fifth year of the trial, I was driving down the highway traveling to a meeting. I was crying out to God and finding my praise for Him within my heart, when suddenly I felt a breakthrough in the Spirit. I can't really explain it except to say that I knew that I knew that I knew, the trial of our faith was over and the breakthrough had come! Within the next couple of weeks there was breakthrough after breakthrough after breakthrough in our finances, and we were catapulted into a whole new level of operative anointing and authority in the Spirit.

Within a short time after that breakthrough, the Lord gave us a new assignment and sent us to Tijuana, Mexico, to minister to the poorest of the poor. Over 80% of the city's population lived in dire poverty at that time. We were untouched by the spirit of poverty and lack in the region during our three and half year ministry season there. We prospered greatly and therefore were able to bless the poor and various Mexican ministries in the area.

We are blessed so that we can be a blessing. We started with nothing and believed the Lord for a small team of people who were willing to live by faith. We left on our journey to Mexico with a team of eight adventurous young adults, a van that someone donated to us just prior to us leaving, a box of kitchen supplies, a box of office supplies, and $1200 in cash that we had collected in outreach fees.

Despise not the days of small beginnings! Every day we believed God, and our provision grew exponentially in a land plagued with poverty. We defied the poverty spirit in the city and fed and clothed the poor every day, built houses for the homeless, and aided in the building of orphanages and medical centers. We reaped a large harvest of souls and witnessed God's miracle power in healing, deliverance, and provisional intervention in amazing ways. We prospered in the midst of poverty. Poverty and lack, although all around us, could not touch us. We were living in The Zone!

As I look back, I have only praise and thanksgiving. He preserved us all those years in the wilderness before our breakthrough. There wasn't a day when we went to bed without something to eat. We were never naked, but clothed. We always had a roof over our heads and every bill was paid. We actually lacked nothing. His presence became more than enough for us. He is truly all we need. He *is* Blessing itself. Following the grueling period of trial and testing was an enormous promotion into the blessings of God – not just for us but also for a city, a nation. That season of working our faith muscles and testing our commitment to God prepared us to walk in greater blessings than we could ever have imagined.

Carve Out a Place of Victory

You carve out a permanent place of victory through standing on the Word of God with unshakable faith and passing all the faith tests for that level. It is worth it all. It is a true gift to receive the reward of perseverance. That same breakthrough and established portal of financial blessing we secured over 20 years ago is still established in our lives today. In those days, we believed for thousands of dollars to help the poor. Today our ministry believes for millions. It is the same God of breakthrough. It is the same God of provision and blessing. "He is good, for His lovingkindness is everlasting" (Psalm 136:1). "After you have suffered for a little while, the God of all grace, who called you to His eternal glory in Christ, will Himself perfect, confirm, strengthen and establish you" (1 Peter 5:10).

We learned to believe for supernatural provision on a daily basis in our five-year trial period. Those five years birthed such a blessing realm for us, although we did not recognize the blessing of it all at the time. It was a blessing in disguise. We chose to only receive the promises of God and resisted the lies of the enemy and the lack and poverty he offered. It paid off – big time! Our faith measure accelerated beyond belief at that time and carved out a place of victory for us that cannot be stolen by the enemy, for this place is in Christ.

THE BEATITUDES

The Beatitudes give you a glimpse into some of the blessings that are promised you – blessings in disguise.

The Blessing of Being Poor in Spirit.

"Blessed are the poor in spirit, for theirs is the kingdom of heaven" (Matthew 5:3).

There are times in life when you feel spiritually empty and dry. I remember a season when I was very spiritually depleted. I had been neglecting my devotional and personal worship times with the Lord due to becoming overly consumed with practical ministry administration and oversight. I ran on old fuel for a while and ended up dull and empty in spirit. As a result of my negligence in seeking the Lord, I began to lean on my own understanding in decision-making and in completing assignments. My lack of abiding in Christ affected my view of life, my faith, and my level of joy. Everything became an effort for me rather than being found in the midst of His glorious grace that enables. I was indeed poor in spirit. You might think, "Well, how could that be a blessing?"

When you live in The Zone, everything turns into a blessing even if your situation looks devastating. Your trials can potentially be a stumbling block for you or a stepping-stone. Your failures can be a curse or they can turn into a blessing depending on your perspective and the actions you take. Life in the blessing zone is amazing because once you determine that only blessings are allowed in your sphere of life, then everything turns into a blessing even if it didn't look like one to begin with.

The greatest blessing for me at that time was to have a firsthand encounter with the reality of the weakness of my carnal nature. In Matthew 26:33, Peter said to Jesus, "Even though all may fall away because of You, I will never fall away." Peter did not know the strength of his carnal nature and he relied on his own self more than he realized.

He did indeed deny the Lord following his bold confession of loyalty and as a result was devastated. Jesus restored broken and disillusioned Peter, but it was not until Peter was completely broken and poor in spirit that the door opened for him to step into the full blessing of his destiny. He needed to see his own weakness or poverty of spirit so that he would not rely on himself when the Lord set him in place to be one of the most strategically positioned apostles in church history. You can trust someone who knows his own weakness and has learned to overcome. Some of your most valuable lessons in life will be learned through some of your greatest failures.

A wild stallion in the field is beautiful to look at, but useless for service until it is broken. It needs to yield to its trainer, but cannot do so until its own will is broken. Peter needed to see the weakness of his own flesh so that he could be completely dependent on the grace of God. Jesus said that you are blessed when you are poor (needy, empty) in spirit, for the kingdom of heaven is yours in that place of acknowledgement. When you are empty, then you can see the beauty and reality of Kingdom life in Christ.

When I was poor in spirit, I turned to God more than ever because I knew that He alone could fill me. I couldn't fix the problem with any carnal solutions – only turning towards God could give me my breakthrough. In my desperation, I truly did seek the Lord and cried out to Him for breakthrough. As I poured my heart before Him in love, expectation and faith, my need was more than met. He revealed to me how I had stepped off the path of single-focused devotion, He led me to repentance and brokenness, and then filled me with increased revelation of Himself, His kingdom, and His righteousness. My poverty of spirit did not look like a blessing, but it was in fact what took me much deeper into the Lord's heart and ways. I went to a whole new place due to being desperate. "Blessed are the poor in spirit, for theirs is the kingdom of heaven" (Matthew 5:3). Oh, how I love the discipline of the Lord!

The Blessing of Mourning

"Blessed are those who mourn, for they shall be comforted" (Matthew 5:4).

Part of living is dying. If you believe in Christ, then you never die but simply step into the fullness of eternal life as you leave the temporal dimension. However, in the temporal realm you experience termination of life. This means that as long as you are in the world you will suffer loss.

Suffering doesn't always feel good and is not usually equated with a blessing, and yet Jesus Himself said that you are blessed when you mourn. Mourning is a response to loss. If you have never experienced suffering, loss, and mourning then you would never fully understand His comfort.

Often we think of the death of a loved one when we refer to mourning, but other things can die, too. Expectations, opportunities, marriages, dreams, desires and relationships. All these death experiences in the temporal realm can produce a weight of glory for you. During these times, you will become introduced to the Comforter Himself. You will know comfort, and that is a blessing! We seldom look for blessing in the midst of our mourning, but if we do, we will find it. Jesus promised.

The Blessing of Hunger and Thirst

"Blessed are those who hunger and thirst for righteousness, for they shall be satisfied" (Matthew 5:6).

Have you ever felt thankful for where you are in your Christian walk, but your experience in Christ's presence simply makes you hungry and thirsty for more? It unsettles and sometimes even discourages? It is the same in the natural. Hunger is uncomfortable UNTIL you eat. Then you are blessed and satisfied.

Your spiritual hunger and thirst are a blessing for you. You shall be filled with what you hunger and thirst for. This is the blessing! As soon as you identify hunger and thirst, rejoice, because that is your sign that fulfillment is right around the corner.

If you lack appetite, you cannot eat. Individuals have actually died from anorexia. Your body needs food in order to give you the fuel to live, work, and play. If you do not feed your body, you will not live. It is the same in the spiritual dimension. If you do not feed yourself with good spiritual food, you will wither and not have a quality life. But, you cannot eat if you lack appetite. When you acknowledge your hunger, then go the buffet table of His promises and eat up. All His blessings are righteous, so eat to the full and be gloriously satisfied!

Jesus said, "If anyone is thirsty, let him come to Me and drink" (John 7:37). Jesus always meant what He said and said what He meant. If you are thirsty for more of Him, for more revelation, for refreshment in His presence, then go to Him and receive. Drink of the pure water of the Word and the Spirit. Drink of the pure river of life that flows from the throne in heaven.

In the Zone, you don't have to wait to be invited to His banqueting table – you were already invited two thousand years ago. You can feast at the table of promises and drink from the fountain of life any time you wish. It is your privilege as a child of God!

If you are hungry – you are blessed. If you are thirsty – you are blessed. Why? Because you will be filled!

The Blessing of Persecution.

"Blessed are those who have been persecuted for the sake of righteousness, for theirs is the kingdom of heaven. Blessed are you when people insult you and persecute you, and falsely say all kinds of evil against you because of Me. Rejoice and be glad, for your reward in heaven is great..." (Matthew 5:10-12).

When people are speaking evil of you, believe me, it does not initially feel like a blessing at all. Each of us has been created for acceptance and not rejection. Persecution, slander, and evil speaking are hurtful and yet the Word unmistakably says that when we are persecuted for His name's sake, and when people speak evil against us falsely, then we are blessed, and we even receive a great reward in heaven.

I remember the first morning after receiving Christ. My heart was so full of joy for being forgiven! I had been emotionally unsettled and ready to be institutionalized, and now Jesus had set me free. I went door-to-door in my neighborhood. I was so excited, and I thought that the only reason people had not received Jesus yet was because they did not know. I knocked on my neighbors' doors and when they answered, I excitedly shared the good news. I said, "Last night, Jesus came into my heart and removed all my sin, and He can remove yours, too. Would you like that?" I will never forget the look on the face of the first couple that came to the door. They responded by saying, "Have you gone crazy?" I replied spontaneously, "No, I was crazy but now I'm not crazy." They looked at me perplexed and with disgust and certainly let me know that they were not interested. I received similar responses at other homes, although most were more polite.

Within a few days, the word had spread around the neighborhood that I had lost my mind. (Praise the Lord, I actually had! The Lord gave me His in exchange.) The report came back to me that slanderous rumors were going around the neighborhood and that I was now labeled as a religious fanatic. This was my introduction to controversy and it hasn't stopped. As a forerunner, I have experienced persecution and slander in every conceivable way you can imagine. It is never comfortable or pleasant and almost always hurts; yet the Lord calls it a blessing.

As a brand new baby Christian I was scorned and mocked by my neighbors. Shame tried to come on me when I heard the gossip, but the same day I received the report, the Holy Spirit quickened to me Matthew 5:12. I was amazed at His promise. I was so in love with Jesus that the promise of eternal blessing far outweighed the persecution and reviling. It was my introduction to learning how to pass love tests. I chose to humble myself before God, bask in His love and trust Him for the reward He promised. I had been forgiven of so much, it was easy for me to forgive others.

I had been loved so unconditionally and now I got to be like Jesus by choosing to return that same love to those who were hurting me. I went quiet without a defensive reaction and just loved.

I grew quickly in the Lord as a baby in Christ and the neighborhood persecution worked to separate my heart even more to God and to overcome the fear of man. I am called to live before an audience of One. I learned to love when I wasn't loved. I learned to forgive when mistreated. I learned to bless those who cursed me. What an awesome reward!

Years later, my husband and I had planted a church and apostolic center. A three-year outpouring of the Spirit filled our ministry and influenced our region. Our apostolic leaders had blessed our church plant but the city leaders had not. They did not like the renewal we were experiencing and they let us know. They preached warnings about us from their pulpits and Christian pastors spoke curses against us.

One day, the head of the ministerial came to visit me and let me know face-to-face that he and the others in the ministerial were standing against me and our church. I listened to his heart and humbled myself without getting self-protective. He told me not to bother to come to the ministerial meetings, as they did not want me there. I thanked him for his honesty but gently informed him that I would continue to serve the ministerial. I also thanked him for setting me up for great reward in heaven. I am not sure he was happy about that, but I will make sure he gets the credit for my reward because I actually did nothing to warrant it. It simply comes as a result of being persecuted and for having people speak evil against you falsely. Our church was actually the most faithful church to the ministerial gatherings and assignments. In the ministers' meetings, I would sit still and silent most of the time (except when I got up to pour their coffee and serve them donuts – they liked that). I listened, I prayed, I encouraged, I blessed.

Following that season, the Lord led us on and opened up a global platform of itinerant ministry. Every time we have experienced a season of persecution and slander, we get promoted, and blessing comes upon us.

I never find these seasons comfortable. Some of them are extremely painful, but they all lead me closer to His heart and call me into deeper levels of humility before God and man. These seasons of persecution and slander test my love levels so that I can "partake of Christ's sufferings" (1 Peter 4:13 NKJV).

When you live in The Zone, everything turns into a blessing. I know this! When the devil assaults you, he intends to harm and destroy you and your faith. And his assaults will do just that if you let them. But when you are committed to blessing, each assault will turn into goodness for you. Blessings in disguise are all around you. I always tell the devil when he comes with attacks, "You will be sorry you ever tried!" I say this with confidence because Jesus promises me victory in all things. Intended evil will turn to good for me. I am blessed in all things. So are you. Live in The Zone!

CHAPTER

4

POSITIONED FOR BLESSING

Blessed be the God and Father of our Lord Jesus Christ,
who has blessed us with every spiritual blessing
in the heavenly places in Christ.
Ephesians 1:3

You are created to live in The Zone. Living in all the blessings granted you in Christ is your portion in life. This chapter is about positioning yourself to experience perpetual blessing. Once you are positioned, blessings will come upon you and overtake you. When you are in a posture to receive, even the adverse situations that come your way turn into blessings for you. What a glorious life! The following is a review of various aspects concerning life in The Zone so that the truths will be clear and established in your heart and mind.

UNDERSTAND WHO YOU ARE IN CHRIST

In Christ you are a new creation. When you are born again you immediately become a recipient of every promise in the Word of God. This is because Jesus made a covenant with God on your behalf and fulfilled all righteousness. You are blessed because you are in Christ.

You are now a child of the Living God. You are His ambassador in the earth. You are a king and priest unto Him. You are more than a conqueror. You are the head and not the tail, above and not beneath. You can do all things through Christ who strengthens you.

Whatever you focus on, you empower. Therefore, if you focus on who you are in Christ, then you will empower the promises of your covenant in Him. If you focus on your shortcomings and the weakness and longings of your carnal nature, then you will empower those things. Know who you are! Remember who you are!

A friend of mine shared a story with me about a tribe in Africa. When a woman discovered that she was pregnant, she would go away by herself into the bush and wait for a song to be birthed in her heart for her child. The song proclaimed the child's destiny and gifts. The mother would then go back to the village and teach everyone the song. When she delivered the child, the villagers would rally around her. The entire village would sing the song over the child during the delivery. The child was literally born into his song of destiny. As they grew up and needed discipline, the mother would take the child into a quiet place and sing the song over the child again. This caused the child to once again focus on who she was. I love this story!

It is so important to think right. "For as he thinks in his heart, so is he" (Proverbs 23:7 NKJV). Renew your mind according to the truth. You are a new creation in Christ. Whatever the Word says you are, you are. Whatever the Word says you have, you have.

ALIGNMENT TO THE WORD AND WAYS OF GOD

It is vital that you align with God's Word and His ways if you are to receive His blessings. It is wise to obey God's Word and it is foolish to disobey. "Do not be deceived, God is not mocked; for whatever a man sows, this he will also reap. For the one who sows to his own flesh will from the flesh reap corruption, but the one who sows to the Spirit will from the Spirit reap eternal life" (Galatians 6:7,8). You cannot expect to live contrary to God's ways and remain in the blessings. A kingdom is the domain and rule of a king. If you live in the domain of King Jesus, you will live in the blessings of His kingdom.

If you spend time in the Word of God every day, the Word will guard your steps and keep you in the truth. I love the book of Proverbs and read through it often. It contains so many practical guidelines and instructions for life, but it also has the most references to wisdom. I grow in wisdom by reading the book of Proverbs because the Word does not return void but accomplishes everything it is sent to do. The words regarding wisdom are imparted into my soul and go to work for me. When you have wisdom, you have blessings.

Divine order brings divine glory. Align with the Word of God and His righteousness. Align with His ways and live in The Zone. Many people want to claim the blessings by faith but do not understand the alignment needed to act on the Word of God. Without works our faith is dead.

THE POWER OF EXPECTATION

I have discovered that when you have expectation for blessings, blessings come. I like to take time each day and dream for a while. I like to meditate on the goodness of God and allow expectation for His blessings to bubble up within me. Invariably what I delight in and joyfully expect seems to come to pass.

What expectations do you have? Some people always expect the worst and so they get the worst. Those who expect the best usually get the best on a continual basis.

Expect blessings every day. Throughout your day remind yourself that you are blessed. Expect favor. Expect open doors. Expect financial blessings. Expect great relationships. Expect breakthroughs and victories. Expect increase. You will receive what you expect. Expectation attracts what you are expecting.

Recently I have been practicing expectation with great deliberation. For example, one day as I was checking in for a flight, I realized that the trip home was almost four hours and I was in a crowded economy seat. I allowed an expectation for upgrade to rise up within my heart. I asked the ticket agent if there were any other seating options. They looked through their system and found the perfect seat – an upgrade to an exit row, which happened to have even more legroom than first class. My expectation for upgrade opened the door for it.

I am not saying that I always see my expectation fulfilled, but I do find that the more I expect blessings, the more they come. Sometimes when we suffer disappointment because our hope has been deferred, we don't bother to expect good again. We rationalize the situation and think, "If I don't expect good, then I won't be disappointed if it doesn't happen." That kind of thinking is of course inspired by "the spirit of stupid."

If you don't expect good, then good will not manifest. If you have fallen into disappointment, get up on your feet and keep moving forward. If you fall into disappointment again, then get up again. Do not give up on expecting blessings and good things in life. Keep moving forward in your expectations until blessings literally come upon you and overtake you. Let waves of blessings wash over you. As you sow expectation you will reap what you expect. Those who live in The Zone live in expectation of good things.

RENEWING THE MIND

The Scripture teaches us that the carnal nature is at enmity against God. "Because the carnal mind is enmity against God; for it is not subject to the law of God, nor indeed can be" (Romans 8:7 NKJV). Therefore if you do not renew your mind according to the truth, you will lean to your own understanding. You renew your mind through the Word of God. Every time you read and meditate on the Word of God, your mind is washed and renewed in the ways of the Kingdom.

Your circumstances are based on facts, and facts are of the temporal realm. Facts are subject to change. The Scripture is inspired by the Spirit of Truth and truth is of the eternal realm. Truth is unchangeable. Your mind must be renewed according to truth in order to enjoy living perpetually in the blessings of God.

Our minds naturally tend to lean towards negativity and fear. When we meditate on the Word we are renewed in the truth and are postured to receive blessings.

ATTITUDE AND PERSPECTIVE ARE EVERYTHING!

Those who live in The Zone have attitudes and perspectives based on faith and positive outcomes. Your attitude and perspective towards life will often determine what kind of life you actually have.

You have probably met people who are negative about everything. They can be blessed in many areas of their life but they will focus on the areas where they aren't blessed rather than where they are. If their cup were filled halfway with water, they would probably view it as half empty rather than half full.

A good attitude and perspective will attract blessings. Always look for the good in everything. Philippians 4:4-9 says,

"Rejoice in the Lord always; again I will say, rejoice! Let your gentle spirit be known to all men. The Lord is near. Be anxious for nothing, but in everything by prayer and supplication with thanksgiving let your requests be made known to God. And the peace of God, which surpasses all comprehension, will guard your hearts and your minds in Christ Jesus. Finally, brethren, whatever is true, whatever is honorable, whatever is right, whatever is pure, whatever is lovely, whatever is of good repute, if there is any excellence and if anything worthy of praise, dwell on these things. The things you have learned and received and heard and seen in me, practice these things, and the God of peace will be with you."

In other words, you are to always look to the good. Always find the "silver lining in every cloud."

Once I had a goal for a certain amount of return on a project. For the sake of this example, let's say the return expected was 100 units. After laboring on this project for a number of days I finally got a breakthrough. The crack in the door opened for fulfillment. I pressed in, labored hard, and received my first return. I met with my other team members right away to share the good news, as we had been pressing in together. I was so excited about the breakthrough!

They asked me how many units my breakthrough had produced. I figured it out quickly in my head and excitedly said, FIVE! They looked at me, shocked, then looked at each other and laughed. They said, Patricia, we need 100 units. I responded, "I know, we only have 95 more to go." It is all about attitude and perspective. We continued to rejoice in every little breakthrough and eventually increased until the fulfillment of our goal was met.

When I first became a Christian, I loved the hymn, "Count your blessings, name them one by one." When you think on all the ways you are blessed, it gives you a clear perspective of your life in The Zone. To this day, I often like to go to sleep thinking about how blessed I am.

If you have a positive perspective, you will attract positive things. If you have a negative attitude and perspective you will attract the negative. I have seen this over and over again. I have known individuals that were actually financially blessed but they did not have that perspective. They always looked at what they didn't have rather than what they had. They compared themselves with others who had more than they did. They failed to see how much the Father had blessed them. They were always disgruntled and lived in a poverty and lack mentality even though they had more than enough.

On the other hand I have known people who had very few earthly things and yet praised the Lord always for how blessed they were. They were thankful for everything they had and lived in the attitude and perspective of blessing… they were blessed indeed!

ONLY BELIEVE

Jesus said, "All things are possible to him who believes" (Mark 9:23). We have already covered the importance of faith, but this cannot be stressed enough. Living in the fullness of the blessings of Christ cannot be secured without faith. Faith is your downloader. Faith is your connector. Faith is your heavenly currency.

When the Holy Spirit quickens a promise to you in the Word, He expects you to embrace it and receive it into your heart and life. He wants you to enjoy the benefit of it. Lock into the promise like a dog with a bone and don't let go until it comes into manifestation. As I mentioned earlier, when you receive a promise, it is like becoming pregnant. The moment faith comes, you have the substance or the reality of the promise within you. It will grow just like a baby does in the womb and one day you will see the manifestation of it, but while you are waiting you still have it. Live like you do. ONLY believe.

Doubt and unbelief are extremely dangerous. Israel could not enter into their promised land because of unbelief, even though the promise remained. In the book of James we are taught that if we doubt, we will receive nothing from the Lord (see James 1:6-8). ONLY believe.

Determine Your Zone

This cannot be stressed enough. You are the one who chooses blessing or curse for your life. The decision is yours. Make a quality decision today to live ONLY in the blessings of God. Don't just ponder it in your heart, but deliberately choose and establish your blessing perimeter. It is your determination and choice that sets your perimeter in place. You simply make the decision in your heart and then proclaim it with your mouth. Decree, "I will live ONLY in the blessings of God. I live in The Zone of His goodness." If anything tries to assault you that is not a blessing, you address it and say, "Only blessings come into my life, therefore, you will turn into a great blessing for me."

It helps me when I write out my decrees and choices in journals, on notes in my Bibles, or even on my fridge, computer, desk etc. Keep the vision of living in The Zone before you, so you remember who you are and what you have. That way you will stay focused, and whatever you focus on you will empower.

Prayer

"You do not have because you do not ask" (James 4:2). Oftentimes, you do not experience fullness of blessing because you do not ask. First John 5:14,15 teaches us that "If we ask anything according to His will, He hears us. And if we know that He hears us in whatever we ask, we know that we have the requests which we have asked from Him."

In Mark 11:24 Jesus taught that all things that we pray and ask, we are to believe that we have received them, and they will be granted. You are exhorted through the Scripture to pray so that your joy may be full. If you desire blessings, ask for blessings according to the will of God and they shall be granted you. The Word clearly teaches this.

Prayerlessness is often the reason why we fall short of what the Lord desires to give us. I love contending in prayer for breakthrough. Then keep a record of answered prayers, too. It will encourage you.

I remember waking up with the flu one morning. It was attacking my body. I was suffering with a headache, sore muscles and joints, and was nauseated. Instead of going right to prayer when I acknowledged the symptoms, I entered into self pity and whining. I said, "Oh no, I'm sick." With that acknowledgement I empowered the sickness in my body and sealed it into my system. Sickness is not a blessing and it doesn't belong to my life in The Zone, but I fully invited it in.

My husband declared, "You are NOT sick! You are healed in Jesus' name! You have the blessing of divine health!" With that declaration of faith I realized that I had failed to pray for healing to enter my body. Instead of asking for a blessing and receiving it by faith, I acknowledged the sickness. I was ready to take a Tylenol before I even prayed to ask the Lord for His wisdom. I received from my own understanding instead of receiving the blessing of healing through prayer.

I realized what I had done and immediately came into agreement with God's Word. I prayed and received my healing. I continued to fight the good fight of faith that day and established my blessing perimeter. It took a while before the full manifestation of the healing came, but in the meantime I had set the perimeter and established The Zone. I locked in through prayer and decree and followed the Lord into a glorious release of His health and strength.

Life in The Zone is amazing and it is for you! Your entire life can and will increase in blessing as you follow the Lord. You were created for this, so go for it!

PART TWO

CHAPTER

5

YOU ARE BLESSED

WITH FAVOR

*For it is You who blesses the righteous man, O LORD,
You surround him with favor as with a shield.*
Psalm 5:12

Jesus grew in favor with God and man; that same increasing and sustained favor is yours when you are in Christ. I have experienced both favor and rejection and, like you, I like favor much better! When you are favored, doors open for you, people like you and don't necessarily even know why. Goodness is attracted to you, everything "comes up roses," and amazing opportunities are always at your doorstep. When you experience favor, there is a skip in your step and you are literally energized by it.

A number of years ago, I read a little booklet called FAVOR. I was so inspired through it that I started believing for increased favor, and it was exciting to see how quickly favor came to me when I started anticipating it. I studied scriptural promises on the favor that had been granted me in Christ. I confessed them on a daily basis, believing that they would manifest in my life… and they did!

It was like stepping into a life-giving current of the undeserved, unmerited, favor of God. I would stand in long grocery store or bank lines and suddenly another counter opened up. One time a teller who had just opened up, pointed right at me, saying, "Let me help you over here, ma'am." There were others in front of me but she insisted that she had opened to serve me.

When shopping, I'd get discounts on items without even asking. I was upgraded on flights and car rentals. Doors on the mission field opened up, as well as opportunities in ministry. I would receive special concessions, enormous price breaks, and extra-quality service when buying real estate and vehicles. In the workplace I was given preference regarding vacation schedules, and I received unexpected and unsolicited bonuses. Divine appointments would connect me with favorable associations that granted many opportunities for blessings.

Sometimes I can actually feel the tangible favor. It is like a special glow and an attraction gift. It has rested on me in certain meetings, relational connections, restaurants and airports. Whenever the tangible favor is present, increased anointing and miracles seem to prevail.

Although I've enjoyed all the aforementioned blessings of favor, the most cherished times of blessing for me are when I am on the streets witnessing, and people who do not know Christ favor me. When favor manifests, they are mysteriously drawn to Christ in me like bees to honey. Without favor, we can preach a great gospel message but no one will listen or receive. You need the favor of God in order to win the lost. You need the favor of God in order to influence nations. Favor is awesome!

FAVOR – A POWERFUL WEAPON AGAINST REJECTION

I met a family a number of years ago plagued with a spirit of rejection. I had never heard anything like the horrific stories they shared. They were a family of four (two parents, a son and a daughter). Each member of the family suffered personal rejection and the family itself was rejected. They explained to me how this rejection had been a stronghold for generations. It was very bizarre and also very evident that it was a demonic assignment over their lives.

They explained to me that as a family they were rejected at church, amongst relatives, and in their neighborhood. Both the father and mother complained of rejection in their workplace and in every church they had attended over the years. The children were rejected at school and in their youth group. None of them had any true personal friends – not one. They had fallen into such a victim mentality that they actually expected rejection rather than favor. They seemed like nice enough people, but rejection suffocated them.

When you have a rejection spirit, it is as though there is a name plaque on your forehead that says REJECT ME! You can always tell when there is a spirit of rejection on a person, because you want to reject them. If a person has the spirit of the Lord's favor on them, you want to favor them.

We ministered deliverance to this dear family and broke off some demonic assignments that came through the generation line. I then shared some keys with them:

Reject Rejection. We explained that rejection was not their portion in Christ. Favor was. They could not let rejection into their lives any more. They were to literally reject rejection and not sign for and accept any more packages with contents of rejection.

Receive Favor by Faith. We taught the family to connect to the promises of favor through faith that were in the Word of God.

Expect Favor. They were instructed to expect favor each and every day and to remind themselves often that favor was their portion.

Confess Favor. We gave them some written decrees based on the Word of God to proclaim over their lives each day. They were to always confess favor and never rejection. They were taught to align with the truth and not the facts.

Sow Favor. They were encouraged to sow favor into other people's lives even if the people they sowed into didn't reciprocate. The Word is true and teaches that if you sow bountifully you will reap bountifully. You will! They were to sow favor into people's lives each and every day, with an expectation of return. And the more they sowed the better.

They were also cautioned not to "dig up the seed early" to check it out. Leave it in the ground and give it time to grow and produce. They were to concentrate on the sowing aspect with an expectation of reaping one day. Ecclesiastes 11:6 teaches, "Sow your seed in the morning and do not be idle in the evening, for you do not know whether morning or evening sowing will succeed, or whether both of them alike will be good." Ecclesiastes 11:1 further states that you are to, "Cast your bread on the surface of the waters, for you will find it after many days." The Scripture guarantees a return of favor when you sow favor.

Praise. We taught the family to praise the Lord for His great favor when they felt attacks of rejection and discouragement. God has given us undeserved, unmerited favor and He is worthy of our sacrifice of praise even when it seems things aren't working out for us. Praise changes the atmosphere from rejection to favor.

Confront the Enemy. They were instructed to confront rejection with the power of favor. The favor of God is much more powerful than the devil's rejection. Rejection was their enemy and if it tried to assault them they would not only resist the rejection, firm in their faith, but they would determine they would see the assault bring forth a great testimony. They were taught to flip the assault into a blessing and make the devil sorry he ever tried.

After putting these valuable tools and weapons into their hands, we had a final prayer and then left to travel home. I saw them again three months later. They had seriously applied all the principles of receiving and exercising their God-given blessing of favor. The results were astounding! They were filled with joy and shared numerous testimonies of God's faithfulness. They experienced favor in their community, at their workplace, in their schools and church. One year later I returned to that region again, and they were still enjoying the enormous favor of the Lord. The curse of rejection was broken by the power of favor.

FAVOR DEFINED

Study the following definition of favor and begin to dream of increased levels filling your life. Meditate on each one.

Favor is:

- an act of gracious kindness.

- to prefer or promote over another.

- an advantage given to the benefit of someone or something.

- to consider as the favorite (i.e. "Joseph was the favorite son of his father").

- an inclination to approve.

- to treat gently or carefully.

- a feeling of favorable regard.

- a privilege: to bestow a privilege and benefit upon.

RECEIVING FAVOR BY FAITH

You have already been granted this wonderful blessing of favor. It is yours in Christ. You don't deserve it or warrant it, but it is yours. Accept it in faith. Lay hold of it. As you choose to accept His favor, you will grow in favor with God and with man. Favor is a spiritual substance or blessing that will work for you in many ways. It is yours, but you must receive it by faith. Jesus taught you to receive what you ask for *when* you pray. You actually receive favor into your heart by faith. When you have it by faith, then you literally have it. "Therefore I say to you, all things for which you pray and ask, believe that you have received them, and they will be granted you" (Mark 11:24).

Faith connects the substance of favor to your heart. Your faith brings the invisible blessing of favor out of the heavenly places in Christ into your life. Deliberately receive favor by faith and you shall have favor.

When you have it, then it can grow in you and manifest in your daily life everywhere you go. It is that simple.

EXAMINE YOURSELF

Sometimes there are reasons for not receiving favor. For example, I knew a young man a number of years ago who had very bad breath and such terrible body odor that it made you think you were going to pass out when you were near him! He wore unwashed clothes, spoke with crudeness, and was generally unkempt in appearance. Did he suffer rejection? You bet he did! There were reasons why he didn't get chosen for the jobs he applied for. There were reasons why people did not want to invite him over to their home for dinner or out for fellowship.

If you are rejected, it might not necessarily be a demon of rejection assaulting you or people's insensitivity towards you – it could be your armpits! Wash them, use some deodorant and see what happens.

It is healthy to examine yourself to see if there are offensive ways in you or ways that need an adjustment in your outlook on life. Favor is yours in Christ, but let's align with the things that attract favor and resist the things that don't. Truly humble yourself and invite the Holy Spirit to show you anything He wants to bring into alignment so that you can enjoy the blessings of abundant favor.

WHAT YOU FOCUS ON, YOU EMPOWER

Focus is very powerful and I can guarantee you that if you focus with fervent passion on the promises of God concerning His favor towards you, you will get immersed in favor. Favor will go before you and favor will follow you. You will wake up to favor in the morning. Favor will greet you in your home, the marketplace and workplace. Favor will follow you everywhere you go throughout your day and will hover over you while you sleep at night.

Set your mind on those things that are good and lovely. "Finally, brethren, whatever is true, whatever is honorable, whatever is right, whatever is pure, whatever is lovely, whatever is of good repute, if there is any excellence and if anything worthy of praise, dwell on these things" (Philippians 4:8). Why focus and set your mind on these things? Because when you do, you attract goodness and blessings. Proverbs 23:7 teaches us that as a man thinks in his heart, so is he. Let's stay focused!

THE PERILS OF FAVOR

As with any blessing from God, it is always important that we worship Him with the blessings we receive. It all goes back to Him. Revelation 5:12 confirms this. "Worthy is the Lamb that was slain to receive power and riches and wisdom and might and honor and glory and blessing."

The blessing of favor is granted to us through the goodness of God's love demonstrated through the gift of His Son. It is part of our covenant package. But we must never forget that this blessing of favor is undeserved. It is because of God's mercy alone that we enjoy favor. This must never be forgotten. In our worship we must yield it back up. If people favor us, then we must worship the Lord with that favor and yield it to Him as a gift.

I knew a young man who grew up with terrible rejection and neglect. He had a difficult and painful childhood, and he manifested his pain through outward rebellion, anger and violence. He was incarcerated as a teenager for a serious crime. After serving his sentence, he received Christ and enjoyed a glorious salvation encounter. As he pursued God, more and more blessings came upon him. He lived by the glorious promises of the Word of God. He meditated day and night on the promises, and the blessings continued to multiply in his life. He grew into increased and enormous favor. It was undeserved, unmerited favor, but over time, as the favor continued to multiply, his focus centered on himself and the fame. Pride entered his heart and, like Humpty Dumpty, he had a great fall. His favor crashed and so did his public platform. Pride always comes before a fall.

The favor of God can humble you or produce pride depending on the condition of your heart. You must always remember that favor is undeserved and unmerited! It should always lead you to greater levels of humility when you realize how undeserved it is and how good God is.

Daniel 4 describes the great favor that rested on King Nebuchadnezzar's life. He was granted a glorious Kingdom but did not submit to God in the fear of the Lord. He began to boast and glory in his own accomplishments (see Daniel 4:29,30). Suddenly everything fell – his well-being was diminished to nothing in a moment of time. The king was humbled greatly until he acknowledged the Lord and openly decreed that all the goodness, the glory and the dominion was God's. He was then restored.

Increased favor demands increased humility and worship. Never forget that it is God who is at work in you, both to will and to work for His good pleasure (Philippians 2:13). God gives favor and He deserves the return of it in worship.

THE POWER OF DECREES

I have a firm conviction that the spoken word carves out a path for our lives and that the Word of God goes forth and performs what it is sent to do (see James 3:2-6; Isaiah 55:11). We live by the fruit of our lips – for good or for evil. You will notice that people who always speak negative things about their life usually have a negative and cursed life. Those who proclaim the truth and the blessings of God are usually happy and receive the fruit of their confession. Sowing words of blessings over your life is one of the greatest gifts you can give yourself.

Decree in faith the following simple decree for favor over your life daily and allow the truth to create blessing.

DECREE FOR FAVOR

I am blessed with the undeserved, unmerited favor of the Lord. Favor is a shield around me. I grow in favor with both God and man because my ways delight the Lord and because I love His wisdom and righteousness. I am favored everywhere I go. I am favored in the workplace, the marketplace, my home, my church, and everywhere I go each day. I am favored in relationships. My speech drips with favor.

I am favored in everything I put my hands to. Doors of opportunity open for me, and many blessings are attracted to me because of the undeserved, unmerited favor of the Lord. As I sow favor into the lives of others, I reap a bountiful harvest of favor. Because I sow bountifully, favor comes back onto my life on every wave (see Ecclesiastes 11:1).

Rejection flees from me and has no place to land because favor is my portion. I only receive favor, and every act of disfavor towards me eventually turns into enduring favor on my behalf.

When favor is granted me, I give it back to God in worship and always remember that it is God alone who blesses me with undeserved, unmerited favor. I am humbled by His favor shown towards me. I praise God all the day long because I am greatly favored and greatly blessed.

Scripture Promises – Favor

For it is You who blesses the righteous man, O LORD, You surround him with favor as with a shield. Psalm 5:12

For His anger is but for a moment, His favor is for a lifetime; weeping may last for the night, but a shout of joy comes in the morning. Psalm 30:5

O LORD, by Your favor You have made my mountain to stand strong; You hid Your face, I was dismayed. Psalm 30:7

The rich among the people will seek your favor. Psalm 45:12b

Let the favor of the Lord our God be upon us; and confirm for us the work of our hands; yes, confirm the work of our hands. Psalm 90:17

So you will find favor and good repute in the sight of God and man. Proverbs 3:4

For he who finds me (wisdom) finds life and obtains favor from the LORD. Proverbs 8:35 (amplification added)

He who diligently seeks good seeks favor, but he who seeks evil, evil will come to him. Proverbs 11:27

A good man will obtain favor from the LORD, But He will condemn a man who devises evil. Proverbs 12:2

Good understanding produces favor, but the way of the treacherous is hard. Proverbs 13:15

Many will seek the favor of a generous man, and every man is a friend to him who gives gifts. Proverbs 19:6

A good name is to be more desired than great wealth, favor is better than silver and gold. Proverbs 22:1

And Jesus kept increasing in wisdom and stature, and in favor with God and men. Luke 2:52

For this finds favor, if for the sake of conscience toward God a person bears up under sorrows when suffering unjustly. 1 Peter 2:19

CHAPTER

6

YOU ARE BLESSED
WITH VICTORY

*But thanks be to God, who always leads us in triumph
in Christ, and manifests through us the sweet aroma
of the knowledge of Him in every place.*
2 Corinthians 2:14

You were created to live in peace and well-being, and yet during your life in the realm of time here on earth you experience things that challenge your peace. The enemy of your soul will literally attempt to invade your blessing zone. It is only in the realm of time that you will ever encounter such warfare. When your life in this realm is finished and you step into your eternal home, you will never have anything to resist your faith, peace, blessings, or love again.

When you look at it with that perspective, it makes your struggles and wrestling here on earth extremely special. You only have this one opportunity for the short time you are here to actually know what victory feels like. In heaven there is no resistance and therefore nothing to win. How can you be a winner if there is no race? How can you feel like a true champion and encounter victory if there is no fight?

What is so amazing is that you are promised victory in Christ in all things. No matter what comes against you, God has your back and you win, if you do not give up. He is cheering you on. The great cloud of witnesses is cheering you on. The battle is never over until it's over and it is not over until you win. There is a real thief and he does come to steal, kill and destroy, but you have conquered him through Christ. His weapons cannot prosper against you. No weapon can. The greater his assault against you, the greater your victory. The Lord will always raise up His standard of victory against the assaults of the enemy.

Jesus cut an eternal, unbreakable, covenant between God and man through His finished work on the cross. This has granted you unlimited access into the blessings of God. After Christ's death on the cross He descended into hell and took the full victory over hell, death and the grave (see Revelation 1:18; Ephesians 4:9,10). He has the keys and He has given them to you (see Matthew 28:18; 16:18,19). Christ has triumphed over all and for all time. "When He had disarmed the rulers and authorities, He made a public display of them, having triumphed over them through Him" (Colossians 2:15). His triumph is your triumph. His victory is your victory.

When you face a trial, immediately begin to rejoice in the coming victory. I always say, "Devil, you will be sorry you ever tried!" I say this with absolute confidence because I know that I always have the victory in Christ. I don't always understand how the Lord is going to work everything out, but I know He is going to. I win! He promised!

Rise up in faith and assuredness when you are hit with a bomb from the enemy. The Lord will work it together for good for you. Lock in to your victory and do not lose sight of the truth. Remember – you win! This is the benefit you receive by living in the blessing zone.

THE POWER OF ENDURANCE

Winners never quit and quitters never win! Galatians 6:9 exhorts us, "Let us not lose heart in doing good, for in due time we will reap if we do not grow weary." When you are at the end of your rope, tie a knot and hang on. Look at what the Bible says about endurance:

"For you have need of endurance, so that when you have done the will of God, you may receive what was promised" (Hebrews 10:36).

"Therefore, since we have so great a cloud of witnesses surrounding us, let us also lay aside every encumbrance and the sin which so easily entangles us, and let us run with endurance the race that is set before us" (Hebrews 12:1).

"Consider it all joy, my brethren, when you encounter various trials, knowing that the testing of your faith produces endurance. And let endurance have its perfect result, so that you may be perfect and complete, lacking in nothing" (James 1:2-4).

"We count those blessed who endured. You have heard of the endurance of Job and have seen the outcome of the Lord's dealings, that the Lord is full of compassion and is merciful" (James 5:11).

THE MIRACLE RELEASING POWER OF PRAISE

When you live in The Zone, you have access to all you need in order to secure victory. Battles, trials and assaults can be very uncomfortable, but they are a perfect setup for the manifestation of miracles. When a storm cloud of tumult comes towards you, start praising the Lord, for His intervention is found in the midst of your praise. I love the story of Jehoshaphat, when Judah was surrounded by three armies (see 2 Chronicles 20:1-30). This situation in the natural was hopeless. The Lord promised them that the battle was His and they were not to fear. They rallied together and praised and worshiped the Lord. Miracle intervention took place while they were in the midst of praise. The Lord turned the three armies against each other, He saved Judah and peace came back to the land.

There are times when the problem is so great that there is nothing in the natural you can do to overcome. Praise Him with all your heart until the breakthrough comes! Praise releases your victory. While you praise, the Lord will fight for you. Miracle breakthrough will come and you will have one more testimony to the glory of God. The victory is yours in Christ!

A number of years ago, I was traveling with a team of young people to Mexico for an outreach. Our vehicle broke down on the way and there was no one in sight to help us. We got out to see what we could do, but none of us had the insight or ability to repair the vehicle. We were stuck and helpless. We needed a miracle, so we started to praise the Lord and thank Him for His goodness. After just a few short moments of praise, a truck pulled over. The driver happened to be a mechanic and was able to diagnose our problem and fix it. The praise brought the intervention and victory.

WHOSE LANDING STRIP?

"Zoners" live their lives for the glory of God. They give the Dove (Holy Spirit) a place to land in their lives. One time during a prayer retreat I asked the Lord to teach me what He liked and what He disliked. I told Him that I wanted to prepare a beautiful place for Him in my heart and life with everything that He loved. I wanted Him to have a true resting place in my life where He would be deeply encouraged and blessed. As a result, I wanted to prepare things that would attract Him and minister to Him.

He revealed to me the things He deeply cherished. Things like unity and love amongst His children, generosity, kindness, faith, care for the poor, widows and orphans, and righteousness. He also revealed to me the things He hated, including discord, slander, pride, selfishness, lies, unbelief, lawlessness, and perversion. I committed to preparing for Him a landing strip in my life, home, and ministry. I truly wanted to attract Him to my heart. He honored my desire, and I constantly am reminded of His glorious presence as it fills my life, home, ministry, and team. He is so good!

The enemy is also looking for landing strips. He is a legalist and if we sin, he will claim his legal ground and entry into our life. Life in The Zone is not a life of sin but of righteousness. Sin will always open the door for defeat but righteousness is the landing strip for victory. There are grave consequences for sin. Israel always won battles when they were aligned to the commandments of God, but when they violated His Word and instruction they were conquered. We must not build a landing strip for the enemy through acts of sin. We must hate sin with a perfect hatred. The Lord said to Cain in Genesis 4:7b, "Sin is crouching at the door; and its desire is for you, but you must master it." Sin is an invitation for defeat and Zoners flee from it – not out of legalistic pressure or control but out of our of love and wisdom.

Galatians 6:7,8 is to be remembered, "Do not be deceived, God is not mocked; for whatever a man sows, this he will also reap. For the one who sows to his own flesh will from the flesh reap corruption, but the one who sows to the Spirit will from the Spirit reap eternal life."

THE IMPACT DECREES HAVE TO SECURE VICTORY

When you decree the truth, it is like an arrow that pierces the heart of your enemy. But the truth is not merely a weapon, it is also a shield! If the Lord promises you victory, then victory you shall have. Do not sign for any other package! You are an overcomer in this life. His Word says so. Your decrees made in faith secure your victory in the Spirit. The Lord will always honor His Word and cause you to triumph in any assault that comes against you. Decree the truth into the midst of your trial. Decree the truth, letting it pierce the heart of your enemy. You will secure the victory!

Angels are also dispatched through the proclamation of the truth. Psalm 103:20 says, "Bless the Lord, you His angels, mighty in strength, who perform His word, obeying the voice of His word!" When you decree the Lord's Word, you become the voice of His word. The angels perform the word and obey the voice. There are warrior angels who will be dispatched into battle when you decree the word of your triumph.

The following is a personal decree for you to proclaim over your life and any assault you are facing. This decree based on the Word will indeed perform what it is commissioned to do. You win, so proclaim your victory!

DECREE FOR VICTORY

I am a victor and an overcomer through Christ Jesus, who always causes me to triumph in Him. The Lord has made a hedge about me and my house and all that pertains to me. The King of Glory, the Lord strong and mighty, the Lord mighty in battle, contends for my victory. He gives His angels charge over me to bear me up and to keep me from falling. No weapon that is formed against me prospers and I confute every tongue that rises up against me in judgment.

The weapons of my warfare are not carnal but mighty through God to the pulling down of strongholds. I cast down imaginations and every high thing that exalts itself against the knowledge of Christ. I bring every thought captive into obedience to the truth.

Greater is He that is in me than he that is in the world. My God has empowered me to run through a troop of enemies and to leap over any and every wall of resistance.

I am not intimidated by the enemy's lies. He is defeated. For this purpose Christ came into the world, to destroy the works of the evil one. I submit to God and resist the devil. As a result he flees from me in terror. The Lord lives mightily in me and I give the devil no opportunity as I submit to the righteousness of Christ.

In Christ, I am the head and not the tail. I am above and not beneath. A thousand shall fall at my side and ten thousand at my right hand, and none shall touch me. I am seated with Christ in heavenly places, far above all principalities and powers. I have been given power to tread upon serpents and scorpions and over all the power of the enemy, and nothing shall injure me. The enemy cannot oppress me, as I am more than a conqueror through Christ and I overcome by the blood of the Lamb and by the word of my testimony, loving not my life unto death.

Scripture Promises – Victory

Know therefore today that it is the LORD your God who is crossing over before you as a consuming fire. He will destroy them and He will subdue them before you, so that you may drive them out and destroy them quickly, just as the LORD has spoken to you. Deuteronomy 9:3

Blessed are you, O Israel; Who is like you, a people saved by the LORD, Who is the shield of your help And the sword of your majesty! So your enemies will cringe before you, And you will tread upon their high places. Deuteronomy 33:29

Have You not made a hedge about him and his house and all that he has, on every side? You have blessed the work of his hands, and his possessions have increased in the land. Job 1:10

We will sing for joy over your victory, And in the name of our God we will set up our banners. May the LORD fulfill all your petitions. Psalm 20:5

Through God we shall do valiantly, And it is He who will tread down our adversaries. Psalm 60:12

You will tread upon the lion and cobra, The young lion and the serpent you will trample down. Psalm 91:13

O sing to the LORD a new song, For He has done wonderful things, His right hand and His holy arm have gained the victory for Him. Psalm 98:1

Through God we will do valiantly, And it is He who shall tread down our adversaries. Psalm 108:13

Where there is no guidance the people fall, But in abundance of counselors there is victory. Proverbs 11:14

The horse is prepared for the day of battle, But victory belongs to the LORD. Proverbs 21:31

For by wise guidance you will wage war, And in abundance of counselors there is victory. Proverbs 24:6

"No weapon that is formed against you will prosper; and every tongue that accuses you in judgment you will condemn. This is the heritage of the servants of the LORD, and their vindication is from Me," declares the LORD. Isaiah 54:17

Shout for joy, O daughter of Zion! Shout in triumph, O Israel! Rejoice and exult with all your heart, O daughter of Jerusalem! Zephaniah 3:14

Rejoice greatly, O daughter of Zion! Shout in triumph, O daughter of Jerusalem! Behold, your king is coming to you; He is just and endowed with salvation, Humble, and mounted on a donkey, even on a colt, the foal of a donkey. Zachariah 9:9

"You will tread down the wicked, for they will be ashes under the soles of your feet on the day which I am preparing," says the LORD of hosts. Malachi 4:3

Behold, I have given you authority to tread on serpents and scorpions, and over all the power of the enemy, and nothing will injure you. Luke 10:19

But in all these things we overwhelmingly conquer through Him who loved us. Romans 8:37

But when this perishable will have put on the imperishable, and this mortal will have put on immortality, then will come about the saying that is written, "DEATH IS SWALLOWED UP in victory." 1 Corinthians 15:54.

But thanks be to God, who gives us the victory through our Lord Jesus Christ. 1 Corinthians 15:57

But thanks be to God, who always leads us in triumph in Christ, and manifests through us the sweet aroma of the knowledge of Him in every place. 2 Corinthians 2:14

For the weapons of our warfare are not of the flesh, but divinely powerful for the destruction of fortresses. We are destroying speculations and every lofty thing raised up against the knowledge of God, and we are taking every thought captive to the obedience of Christ. 2 Corinthians 10:4-5

You are from God, little children, and have overcome them; because greater is He who is in you than he who is in the world. 1 John 4:4

For whatever is born of God overcomes the world; and this is the victory that has overcome the world – our faith. 1 John 5:4

And they overcame him because of the blood of the Lamb and because of the word of their testimony, and they did not love their life even when faced with death. Revelation 12:11

YOU ARE BLESSED WITH ABUNDANCE

I came that they may have life, and have it abundantly.
John 10:10b

Abundance means "more than enough." You are called to live in abundance in the Kingdom of God. When God led Israel out of Egypt, He led them out of a land of "not enough." In the wilderness they had "just enough" but their final destination was the land of "more than enough." God wants you to enjoy abundance in everything that is good. Heaven is full of extravagance and abundance. There is no leanness in heaven because the God of Abundance, the God of Plenty, the God of More Than Enough dwells there. Where He dwells there is no leanness. This is the Kingdom life that we have been invited to live in through Christ Jesus who purchased it for us. This is life in The Zone.

Think on this a little. What would your life look like if you were overflowing in every good thing? When you live in abundance, there is so much overflow that you do not have room enough to contain it. I remember when we started laboring on the mission field in Mexico. We started feeding the poor by sharing the little we had of our own. We also gave them our personal clothes. We sowed into the needs and believed for more "seed" to sow.

As we believed, more donations of food and clothing as well as medical and building supplies flooded in. As soon as we received supplies we distributed them to the poor. Our "problem" was that the seed grew exponentially and, before long, truck loads and boat loads of food, clothing and supplies were sent to us on a fairly continual basis. We literally could not give it out fast enough. As a result, we were forced to rent warehouses so we could store it until we could distribute it. The provision was wonderful, but we actually had to say "NO MORE" for a time until we caught up on distributing it all.

Malachi prophesied that the Lord would pour out a blessing that we could not contain (Malachi 3:10). Just like Malachi said, we literally could not contain it. There was great abundance. We have experienced this many times and in many ways. The abundance of the Lord is promised to all believers.

When we pioneered our ministry in Phoenix, Arizona, Ron and I were living in a little 500 square foot trailer in a resort trailer park. We had an 8x10 foot shed on our lot, also. My desk, computer and filing cabinet were in the shed. That was the "ministry office." When Shirley Ross joined me to produce our television programs, she sacrificed living in her prestigious condo in Irvine, California, and moved into the trailer next to us. She set up shop on her kitchen table. Then Rob Hotchkin joined us. He gave up his dream cabin in Montana and also moved to the desert into a trailer in our park. He set up his office on his kitchen table. Steve and Ruthann Fryer moved from Texas and bought a home with a garage not far from us. They invited us to use half the garage for our resource ministry and Steve's graphic design workspace.

Those were our humble beginnings. Within six months we were occupying the Fryers' full three-car garage with our resources, and had nine people on staff. We then bought 4,000 square feet of space (an old church and a 1500 square foot trailer) in Maricopa, Arizona, just a few miles south of Phoenix. We used the church building for the offices and resources. The trailer was empty as it was more space than we needed at the time. Ron and I, Shirley, and Rob all bought houses in the area and worked out of our homes. Within the next 12 months we more than tripled our staff and not only filled both the church and the trailer but bought more land and secured increased workspace. Within three years we had over 40 staff members and three properties.

Everything multiplied. Our ministry became more fruitful, our staff grew, and our outreach to the nations expanded beyond belief. Instead of reaching 10,000 people per week, we were reaching 100 million. ABUNDANCE! We grew from one ministry department to over 15 in three years. ABUNDANCE!

God has promised you abundance and increase in all things. It all started in the garden, "Be fruitful and multiply." It is part of living Kingdom – it is part of living in The Zone. He wants you to increase in every good thing. This is your portion!

Abundance is manifest in many areas of life. For example, you can believe for abundance of friends, abundance of spiritual gifts, abundance of faith, abundance of wisdom, abundance of love. God desires you to pursue all these good things and live in the fullness of them. Go for it! It is God's will for you!

It is interesting that when you engage in scriptural studies on abundance, prosperity, multiplication, and increase, in the majority of cases the Bible speaks of material abundance. Many Christians are embarrassed or feel awkward regarding material abundance. Even though they might enjoy having abundance of provision in their lives, they don't want to outwardly say it or have people think they would like it.

Let's get real here. You are allowed to desire abundance of material possessions. It is biblical. However, the love of money is the root of all evil, and many people fall away from the faith as a result of their affection for it. We must watch over our hearts with all diligence in this respect. Money is a worldly currency. It is man-made and you must not idolize it. God alone is to be worshipped. You always need to be watchful. Paul taught Timothy to be free from the love of money in 1 Timothy 3:3. Hebrews 13:5 states that you are to, "Make sure that your character is free from the love of money."

We are to love God with all our hearts and idolize nothing. We are also to embrace blessing and abundance in all things. God encourages us in this.

Keys for Living in Abundance

Know the God of Abundance

To live in abundance, you must know the God of Abundance – The God of More than Enough. Many Christians live in a mentality of lack. Why? It is mainly because they have not come to know the God of Abundance in a personal way. Many believe God wants them to live in poverty and suffer with never having enough. Others think they will be delivered from the love of money by not having any. This is not true. Most individuals who do not have money or belongings think about them all day long. They worry and fret over them and are actually more consumed in their thoughts regarding money and material things than those who live in abundance.

When you *know* the God of Abundance in a personal and intimate way, everything changes. Your God does not withhold, He is a God who is generous and gives to those who draw close to Him. Psalm 34:10 states, "They who seek the LORD shall not be in want of any good thing." Psalm 84:11 further confirms, "The LORD gives grace and glory; No good thing does He withhold from those who walk uprightly."

You must never worship "things" but you are to fully enjoy everything the hand of the Lord provides. When you meditate on the God of Abundance and worship Him in His glory, then your eyes will be open to see Him and the reality of His abundance. He is truly the God of Plenty. He is indeed the God of More Than Enough. Spend time in His presence and sincerely invite Him to reveal Himself to you in this dimension. Know Him! Your life of abundance in The Zone does not flow primarily out of *what* you know. It is imparted by *Who* you know. Draw close to the God of Abundance and His fullness will definitely fill you to overflowing.

Develop Soul Prosperity

Third John 1:2 says, "Beloved, I pray that in all respects you may prosper and be in good health, just as your soul prospers." John is teaching the right priority here. He is saying that in order to prosper in outward things, the inward state of the heart first needs to prosper.

In the Kingdom of God, things often seem to be upside down. For example, the greatest in the Kingdom is the servant of all; the highest position is the lowest; in order to live, you die. Understanding these kingdom dynamics is part of your soul prospering. A prospering soul is a secure soul, free from fear and anxiety. A prospering soul is at rest. A prospering soul is content.

I have learned that my soul gets fat and flourishes when I humble myself under the mighty hand of God. When I acknowledge the greatness of God and my complete dependency upon Him, I find richness and abundance within. That is when I realize that He is all I need. He is more than enough. I often meditate on that.

If every material thing in this life were to disappear – my finances, home, furniture, vehicles, wardrobe, and personal belongings – would I be content with only my relationship with God to sustain me? I have been tested on this and, although in the natural the process and journey was uncomfortable, I now know that I know that I know that Jesus is more than enough for me. This is when you realize your soul is fat. All your desires and longings are satisfied in Him. When your soul is fat due to every nook and cranny being filled with love for God, then prosperity and health fill other areas of your life. Godliness with contentment is great gain (1 Timothy 6:6). Your contentment is found in knowing He is more than enough. This produces great gain!

Abide in the Vine

Jesus taught that when you abide in the vine you bear much fruit (study John 15:1-8). While meditating on this passage a number of years ago, I imagined a tree with branches. I realized that the branch doesn't grunt and groan in order to produce fruit. It simply abides. It just hangs there attached to the tree. Every Christian is called to bear much fruit. It is what we were made for. God made it so easy for us. All we have to do is hang out in Jesus. Jesus is your life. He is in you and you are in Him. Acknowledge His place in your life and yours in His every day. You are *one*. As you remain connected through your faith and intimacy, you WILL bear abundance of fruit in your life.

Expect Abundance

Your expectation for abundance is clearly a landing strip for God. You will receive what you expect when your expectations are in line with God's purposes.

I was praying with a woman one day who had amazing dreams and desires for freedom and abundance. Her desires were in line with God's Word. There was a problem, though – she had roots of unbelief in her life. She so desired the blessing of God but she kept repeating over and over again through the course of our conversation, "But I am afraid I will be disappointed. What if I don't see the promise fulfilled?" She surely had an expectation, but it was for nothing good to happen. She expected to be disappointed. This woman did not want disappointment but she was expecting it. She will get what she expects if she does not repent and align her expectations with God's purposes. Expect God's Word to be fulfilled in your life. Be joyfully expectant for abundance of every good thing to fill and satisfy you.

Faith

I have shared a great deal on faith already but am purposely being redundant. Often you need to hear the Word over and over again until the light finally turns on. In order to receive abundance you must believe, not just with head knowledge but with the heart. "With the heart a person believes, resulting in righteousness, and with the mouth he confesses, resulting in salvation" (Romans 10:10).

To live in The Zone of abundance, you must believe the Word of God concerning it. If you do not believe, then study the Word over and over again until it comes alive. It is vital. When you are in faith, you "have it." What you believe has become an internal reality. As soon as it is anchored within your heart, you will see the outer mani-festations. Abundance will then become a sustained blessing in your life. Believe!

Sowing

If you want abundance, then Kingdom economy requires that you sow what you desire to reap. It is a very easy principle and the Bible is full of confirma-tion. I have seen it work for many years in every area of my life. God made a perpetual promise in Genesis 8:22, "While the earth remains, Seedtime and harvest… shall not cease." The earth still remains, so the promise is still good. If you sow a seed there will be a corresponding harvest.

The principle of sowing and reaping is very easy to grasp. If I plant bean seeds in a natural garden, I will grow beans (not corn). If I plant many bean seeds, I will reap more beans than if I just planted a few. If I sow my seeds into good, rich soil, I will reap bountifully. When I plant a seed and it grows to a full plant, it has more seed inside of the fruit.

We can apply this illustration to the abundant life we are called to in the Kingdom. For example, if I want abundant friends in my life I must sow friendship abundantly. If I sow abundant prayers into receiving reve-lation of God, I will receive an abundant harvest of revelation, not a har-vest of friends. If I sow abundant finances into good soil, I will receive an abundant harvest of finances, not a harvest of revelation.

The soil that you sow into is also important. I always look for soil that will be conducive to Kingdom advancement. For example, in the area of finance, I look for ministries to sow into that are rich in faith, love and character. When I sow into anointed ministries, I am assured that the seed will be used for Kingdom advancement. I always increase in finance as a re-sult of sowing financial seed, but I also increase in the anointing of the ministry that I sow into. I love Kingdom!

"Now this I say, he who sows sparingly will also reap sparingly, and he who sows bountifully will also reap bountifully. Each one must do just as he has purposed in his heart, not grudgingly or under compulsion, for God loves a cheerful giver. And God is able to make all grace abound to you, so that always having all sufficiency in everything, you may have an abundance for every good deed; as it is written, 'HE SCATTERED ABROAD, HE GAVE TO THE POOR, HIS RIGHTEOUSNESS ENDURES FOREVER.' Now He who supplies seed to the sower and bread for food will supply and multiply your seed for sowing and increase the harvest of your righteousness; you will be enriched in everything for all liberality, which through us is producing thanksgiving to God" (2 Corinthians 9:6-11).

Reaping

Many have grasped the whole idea of sowing and they are faithful sowers. Intentional reaping, however, is also extremely vital in order to be blessed with abundance. What would you think of a farmer who loved to sow but was shy about reaping, or perhaps even resistant to it? He joyfully and abundantly throws his seed out into a field. He says, "Yippee, I LOVE sowing!!! I don't care about the reaping. I just love to sow, Yippee!" If you were an onlooker, you would think he was an absolute lunatic.

Here is another scenario: A farmer faithfully sows seed into his field. It is good ground and the seed grows into an abundant harvest. Harvest time comes and goes. You drive by weekly and watch the neglected harvest rot and die. One day you meet the farmer while shopping in town and ask him why he didn't reap the field. "Oh," he says, "if God wants me to have a harvest, He will give me one. I am just going to be a faithful sower."

What? That makes no sense. God did give him the harvest. It was right in front of his eyes every day, but he failed to put the sickle in the ground and reap.

In a spiritual sense it is the same. You sow by faith and you must also intentionally reap by faith. Many Christians are faithful in sowing but are not aware of reaping. Some are actually resistant. I have heard a few make comments like the farmers in the story above. They will say things like, "If God wants me to have a return on my sowing, He will give it." Or, "I love sowing and sacrificing but I don't care if I get any return." These responses make no sense whatsoever and are definitely not going to bring forth the fruit of abundance. A farmer sows with the intention to reap, and so should you. When you sow faithfully into good ground, a harvest awaits you. Believe for it. Reap in the time of harvest!

Tithing

The Scripture clearly teaches us that the sincere heartfelt offering of the first and the best goes to God. When we honor Him with the first and the best, then heaven opens and benefits bless our life. The tithe (meaning 10%) belongs to the Lord. It was first offered by Abraham to Melchizedek, the High Priest. God was delighted in this act and blessed Abraham. Later, this act was made law so that all of Israel would live in the same blessing as Abraham. In the New Testament we are not under a law to give 10%, but we offer the tithe through the Kingdom love law and give it from the heart. The blessings of the tithe come upon us. Look at the blessings that are promised you as a result of tithing:

"Bring the whole tithe into the storehouse, so that there may be food in My house, and test Me now in this," says the LORD of hosts, "if I will not open for you the windows of heaven and pour out for you a blessing until it overflows. Then I will rebuke the devourer for you, so that it will not destroy the fruits of the ground; nor will your vine in the field cast its grapes," says the LORD of hosts. All the nations will call you blessed, for you shall be a delightful land," says the LORD of hosts (Malachi 3:10-12).

Weed Your Garden

Don't let weeds choke out the abundance of God in your life. Things like worry, fear, care, anxiety, and other sins are like weeds in your garden of abundance. Leave no place for the devil. Keep your garden clean so that only the good seed grows. The way you weed the garden of your life is through repentance. When the Holy Spirit convicts, you are to repent and invite the Lord to forgive. "If we confess our sins, He is faithful and righteous to forgive us our sins and to cleanse us from all unrighteousness" (1 John 1:9). If you want an abundant life, live clean!

THE POWER OF TESTIMONY AND REMEMBRANCE

All throughout Israel's history, the Lord exhorted His people to remember all the things He did for them. They were to pass these testimonies on to their children so that every generation would rejoice in the Lord's goodness and believe in God because of the word of their testimony. In Revelation 12:11 we are taught that we actually overcome by the word of our testimony. The testimony is powerful. Bill Johnson teaches that when you testify of God's goodness, you release Him to do it again. Every time you are blessed with the Lord's abundance, praise Him, and then sow the testimony into the hearts of many. The Lord's abundance of goodness will then increase.

Life in The Zone is a life of goodness in abundance. Establish belief in the Word of God concerning His desire for you to prosper and to be blessed in fullness. Decree the truth about the abundant life you have in Christ.

DECREE FOR ABUNDANCE

My God is a God of abundance and He delights in my prosperity. No good thing does He withhold from me. I acknowledge that I have more than enough in life because He is the God of More than Enough. My God is the God of Plenty. I choose to sow bountifully; therefore I will reap bountifully. I generously give to the Lord, to His people and to the needy as I purpose in my heart to give. I do not give grudgingly or out of compulsion, for my God loves a cheerful giver. God makes abundant grace abound towards me. I always have enough for all things, so that I may abound unto every good work.

The Lord supplies me with seed to sow and with bread for food. He also supplies and multiplies my seed for sowing and increases the harvest of my righteousness. I am enriched in all things unto great abundance.

I bring my tithe unto the Lord. As a result, He opens up the windows of heaven and pours out a blessing for me that there is not room enough to contain. He rebukes the devourer for my sake, so that he does not destroy the fruits of my ground and neither does my vine cast its grapes before the time. All the nations shall call me blessed, for I have a delightful life in Christ.

I remember the Lord my God, for it is He who gives me the power to make wealth, that He may confirm His covenant. I am blessed and favored because Jesus came to give me a life in abundance.

Scripture Promises – Abundance

God blessed them, saying, "Be fruitful and multiply, and fill the waters in the seas, and let birds multiply on the earth." Genesis 1:22

As for you, be fruitful and multiply; populate the earth abundantly and multiply in it. Genesis 9:7

I will establish My covenant between Me and you, and I will multiply you exceedingly. Genesis 17:2

"May God Almighty bless you and make you fruitful and multiply you, that you may become a company of peoples. Genesis 28:3

So I will turn toward you and make you fruitful and multiply you, and I will confirm My covenant with you. Leviticus 26:9

May the LORD, the God of your fathers, increase you a thousand-fold more than you are and bless you, just as He has promised you! Deuteronomy 1:11

O Israel, you should listen and be careful to do it, that it may be well with you and that you may multiply greatly, just as the LORD, the God of your fathers, has promised you, in a land flowing with milk and honey. Deuteronomy 6:3

He will love you and bless you and multiply you; He will also bless the fruit of your womb and the fruit of your ground, your grain and your new wine and your oil, the increase of your herd and the young of your flock, in the land which He swore to your forefathers to give you.
Deuteronomy 7:13

All the commandments that I am commanding you today you shall be careful to do, that you may live and multiply, and go in and possess the land which the LORD swore to give to your forefathers.
Deuteronomy 8:1

The LORD will make you abound in prosperity, in the offspring of your body and in the offspring of your beast and in the produce of your ground, in the land which the LORD swore to your fathers to give you. Deuteronomy 28:11

The LORD your God will bring you into the land which your fathers possessed, and you shall possess it; and He will prosper you and multiply you more than your fathers. Deuteronomy 30:5

Then the LORD your God will prosper you abundantly in all the work of your hand, in the offspring of your body and in the offspring of your cattle and in the produce of your ground, for the LORD will again rejoice over you for good, just as He rejoiced over your fathers. Deuteronomy 30:9

See, I have set before you today life and prosperity, and death and adversity. Deuteronomy 30:15

Then you will prosper, if you are careful to observe the statutes and the ordinances which the LORD commanded Moses concerning Israel. Be strong and courageous, do not fear nor be dismayed. 1 Chronicles 22:13

Let them shout for joy and rejoice, who favor my vindication; and let them say continually, "The LORD be magnified, Who delights in the prosperity of His servant." Psalm 35:27

But the humble will inherit the land and will delight themselves in abundant prosperity. Psalm 37:11

May the LORD give you increase, you and your children. Psalm 115:14

O LORD, do save, we beseech You; o LORD, we beseech You, do send prosperity! Psalm 118:25

"May peace be within your walls, and prosperity within your palaces." Psalm 122:7

I will abundantly bless her provision; I will satisfy her needy with bread. Psalm 132:15

So your barns will be filled with plenty and your vats will overflow with new wine. Proverbs 3:10

Adversity pursues sinners, but the righteous will be rewarded with prosperity. Proverbs 13:21

Then He will give you rain for the seed which you will sow in the ground, and bread from the yield of the ground, and it will be rich and plenteous; on that day your livestock will graze in a roomy pasture. Isaiah 30:23

Behold, My servant will prosper, He will be high and lifted up and greatly exalted. Isaiah 52:13

You will have plenty to eat and be satisfied and praise the name of the LORD your God, who has dealt wondrously with you; then My people will never be put to shame. Joel 2:26

"Bring the whole tithe into the storehouse, so that there may be food in My house, and test Me now in this," says the LORD of hosts, "if I will not open for you the windows of heaven and pour out for you a blessing until it overflows. "Then I will rebuke the devourer for you, so that it will not destroy the fruits of the ground; nor will your vine in the field cast its grapes," says the LORD of hosts. "All the nations will call you blessed, for you shall be a delightful land," says the LORD of hosts. Malachi 3:10-12

The thief comes only to steal and kill and destroy; I came that they may have life, and have it abundantly. John 10:10

And with great power the apostles were giving testimony to the resurrection of the Lord Jesus, and abundant grace was upon them all. For there was not a needy person among them, for all who were owners of land or houses would sell them and bring the proceeds of the sales and lay them at the apostles' feet, and they would be distributed to each as any had need. Acts 4:33-35

Now He who supplies seed to the sower and bread for food will supply and multiply your seed for sowing and increase the harvest of your righteousness. 2 Corinthians 9:10

Beloved, I pray that in all respects you may prosper and be in good health, just as your soul prospers. 3 John 1:2

8

YOU ARE BLESSED
WITH HEALTH AND
STRENGTH

But for you who fear My name, the sun of righteousness
will rise with healing in its wings; and you will go forth
and skip about like calves from the stall.
Malachi 4:2

Heaven is a sickness-free zone! There are no accidents or mishaps there. Everyone is healthy, strong, and vibrant. As we have already studied, we know that Jesus desires us to live on earth as it is in heaven. If there is no sickness in heaven, then let's contend to live in the zone of vibrant health and strength here on the earth. The Israelites were promised strength and vitality each and every day they lived on earth. This is your promise, too. Deuteronomy 33:25 declares, "As thy days, so shall thy strength be" (KJV). It is our portion as Zoners!

Before sin came into the world, there was no sickness, disease or weakness. Adam and Eve lived in the fullness of the glory as they enjoyed unbroken fellowship with God. It was through man's sin that the door was opened to disease, decay, and corruption. We have virus, bacteria, and all manner of sickness and disease today because of man's sin. It opened the door for terrible attacks to assault good people.

In Exodus 15:26, God addressed the subject of healing with Israel and gave us keys for divine health:

And He said, "If you will give earnest heed to the voice of the LORD your God, and do what is right in His sight, and give ear to His commandments, and keep all His statutes, I will put none of the diseases on you which I have put on the Egyptians; for I, the LORD, am your healer."

God set conditions for health. Israel was instructed to give heed to the voice of the Lord, do what was right, and keep His commandments. He said that He would not "put" any of the diseases upon them that He had "put" on the Egyptians if they gave heed to His word and commandments. I do not believe that God "puts" disease on us in the sense of making us sick with an evil disease, for He is holy. I believe He was speaking of the consequences that come as a result of disobedience.

The Scripture says that God hardened Pharaoh's heart. I used to really wonder why God did that. I asked, "Lord, Why did you harden his heart? If you hardened it, he didn't even have a chance to obey You." It was confusing to me until the Lord revealed something important about this. He showed me two substances: a wax candle and a lump of clay. If you allow the sunshine to beam down upon both of them, the sun will have different effects on each. The candle melts and the clay hardens. The sun softens the wax but the sun also hardens the clay. The same sun does both. It is the substance of the wax and the clay that are different. Pharaoh's heart was resistant to the Word and Presence of God. The substance of his heart was rebellious and disobedient. The Presence of God had a different effect on Aaron and Moses. Their hearts were softened. The same God, the same miracles, the same Presence – but different effects. Yes, God hardened Pharaoh's heart, but not purposely.

It is the same with "putting diseases" on people. God has Kingdom laws – spiritual laws that work for all the people all the time. Let's look at the example of the natural law of gravity. God created this law. If someone walked off the edge of a cliff you could actually say, "Gravity killed the person." God made natural, spiritual and moral laws to be followed, and He created the consequences. You could go even further with the gravity situation and say, "God killed the person," because He was the Creator of the law and consequences that worked against the one who walked off the cliff.

Another example is when we hear someone say that God sent someone to hell. God created hell for the devil and his followers, but God provided a way for us to have unbroken, eternal, fellowship with Him.

According to Romans 1:20, He reveals the truth to everyone, and therefore this Scripture says that we are without excuse. So, does God actually send people to hell or do they choose it? He created hell and the law that determines entrance, but we choose if we go or not.

God taught Israel how to stay clear of sickness and disease. Broken laws and principles bring on consequences. God created those consequences. He in fact was saying, "OBEY so that you will not be submitted to the consequences I have created." God's people were to be separated unto Him, and in that place of close fellowship with Him there would be no sickness or disease.

Today, we see much sickness in the earth. This is because there is more sin. Why do good people get attacked? Because sin is in the air! We must learn to live in the Zone of health and strength, for it is our portion, but we must also contend for it through faith and persistence. We must establish a "no-sickness perimeter" around our lives and not compromise our faith. God wants us healthy and strong!

Whenever I resist sickness the moment it attacks me I usually subdue it, but if I ponder it for a while and say things like, "Oh no, I have a headache. I feel sick," then I just signed for the package and it grips me. I let it. The longer I let it in, the harder it is to drive it out. I must believe the Word more than symptoms. I must stand on the truth rather than fact. And I must send those nasty packages back to the devil and not sign for them. The more I practice this tenacious stand of "no-sickness zone" for my life, the more victory I have.

As a born-again believer, you not only have the blessing of living in health and strength all your days, you also have the power to help others. Christ's healing power is in you. Jesus said, "Truly, truly, I say to you, he who believes in Me, the works that I do, he will do also; and greater works than these he will do; because I go to the Father" (John 14:12). He also said that you could lay hands on the sick and they would recover (Mark 16:18). In Matthew 10:1, He sends His disciples to heal the sick. He continues to send His people today.

Christ's healing power and presence is in you. Impart His healing to others. Allow your faith to grow and don't give up if you pray for a few people and don't see results. Keep praying. Keep focusing on the promises and break through into The Zone of His power and presence.

He has given you everything you need. He is your health and your strength. If you feel weak throughout your day, receive His strength by faith. Take a few moments to wait upon the Lord and allow His strength to renew you, and then move forward in confidence and renewed vitality. Strength, health, and healing are all yours in Christ. Lock in to all the promises. They are yours. This is the privilege of those who live in The Zone!

HE SENT FORTH HIS WORD

Psalm 107:20 says, "He sent His word and healed them, and delivered them from their destructions." The Lord has given us His sure promises regarding health, healing and strength. Meditate on the promises of God daily and allow them to be an anchor within your heart. Be immovable in your faith because the Word is so secured within your understanding. Allow the Word to wash over your mind each and every day.

When you decree healing truth based on the Word of God and His powerful promises, the Word goes forth and heals. There is no time or distance in the Spirit. Send forth the Word and it will go forth and do what it is sent to do. The following are decrees based on God's promises that you can decree into your life and home daily. Once they are decreed, they are established in the atmosphere and begin to bring healing and wholeness.

DECREE – HEALTH AND STRENGTH

I am filled with health and strength, for the Lord is the strength of my life. Sickness and disease flee from me and no plague or pestilence comes near my dwelling. The Lord blesses me with health and healing and lets me enjoy abundant peace and security. No weapon of sickness or disease prevails against me because I am in Christ.

If sickness, disease or accidents attempt to attack me, the Son of righteousness arises for me with healing in His wings, and I go out and leap about like a calf released from the stall. When I call for the elders of the church, they anoint me with oil, pray the prayer of faith and I recover. Jesus bore all my sins in His body on the cross so that I might die to sin and live to righteousness, and by His stripes I am healed.

As my days are, so shall my strength be. When I feel weak I find my strength in His joy, for the joy of the Lord is my strength. As I wait upon the Lord, my strength is renewed like the eagles. I run and do not grow weary. I walk and do not faint. I am satisfied with a long, full life and am sustained by the mighty hand of God.

The power of the Lord works mightily within me as I go to lay hands on the sick. They recover in the name of Jesus because He is with me. I proclaim the gospel, and signs and wonders follow. Healing signs become evident. Healing miracles from God bring breakthroughs in the lives of many, and Jesus receives great glory.

I exalt Jesus Christ as my Savior, King, Lord, Healer, and Deliverer. He is my strength and my goodness.

SCRIPTURES – HEALTH AND STRENGTH

For You have girded me with strength for battle; You have subdued under me those who rose up against me. 2 Samuel 22:40

Seek the LORD and His strength; seek His face continually. 1 Chronicles 16:11

Ascribe to the LORD, O families of the peoples, ascribe to the LORD glory and strength. 1 Chronicles 16:28

Then he said to them, "Go, eat of the fat, drink of the sweet, and send portions to him who has nothing prepared; for this day is holy to our Lord. Do not be grieved, for the joy of the LORD is your strength." Nehemiah 8:10

I love You, O LORD, my strength. Psalm 18:1

For You have girded me with strength for battle; You have subdued under me those who rose up against me. Psalm 18:39

The LORD is my strength and my shield; my heart trusts in Him, and I am helped; therefore my heart exults, and with my song I shall thank Him. Psalm 28:7

How blessed is he who considers the helpless; the LORD will deliver him in a day of trouble. The LORD will protect him and keep him alive, and he shall be called blessed upon the earth; and do not give him over to the desire of his enemies. The LORD will sustain him upon his sickbed; in his illness, You restore him to health. Psalm 41:1-3

My son, give attention to my words; incline your ear to my sayings. Do not let them depart from your sight; keep them in the midst of your heart. For they are life to those who find them and health to all their body. Proverbs 4:20-22

He gives strength to the weary, and to him who lacks might He increases power. Isaiah 40:29

Yet those who wait for the LORD will gain new strength; they will mount up with wings like eagles, they will run and not get tired, they will walk and not become weary. Isaiah 40:31

Surely our griefs He Himself bore, and our sorrows He carried; yet we ourselves esteemed Him stricken, smitten of God, and afflicted. But He was pierced through for our transgressions, He was crushed for our iniquities; the chastening for our well-being fell upon Him, and by His scourging we are healed. Isaiah 53:4,5

Behold, I will bring to it health and healing, and I will heal them; and I will reveal to them an abundance of peace and truth. Jeremiah 33:6

But for you who fear My name, the sun of righteousness will rise with healing in its wings; and you will go forth and skip about like calves from the stall. Malachi 4:2

Jesus was going throughout all Galilee, teaching in their synagogues and proclaiming the gospel of the kingdom, and healing every kind of disease and every kind of sickness among the people. Matthew 4:23

Heal the sick, raise the dead, cleanse the lepers, cast out demons. Freely you received, freely give. Matthew 10:8

And they were casting out many demons and were anointing with oil many sick people and healing them. Mark 6:13

While the sun was setting, all those who had any who were sick with various diseases brought them to Him; and laying His hands on each one of them, He was healing them. Luke 4:40

And all the people were trying to touch Him, for power was coming from Him and healing them all. Luke 6:19

And He sent them out to proclaim the kingdom of God and to perform healing. Luke 9:2

You know of Jesus of Nazareth, how God anointed Him with the Holy Spirit and with power, and how He went about doing good and healing all who were oppressed by the devil, for God was with Him. Acts 10:38

Finally, be strong in the Lord and in the strength of His might. Ephesians 6:10

Is anyone among you sick? Then he must call for the elders of the church and they are to pray over him, anointing him with oil in the name of the Lord; and the prayer offered in faith will restore the one who is sick, and the Lord will raise him up, and if he has committed sins, they will be forgiven him. James 5:14,15

Beloved, I pray that in all respects you may prosper and be in good health, just as your soul prospers. 3 John 1:2

9

YOU ARE BLESSED
WITH EVERLASTING LOVE

I have loved you with an everlasting love;
therefore I have drawn you with lovingkindness.
Jeremiah 31:3

The Cross of Jesus Christ is clearly now the central and core message of my life, but for years I never really understood the significance of it. I knew that Christ died on the cross for my sins but did not have a true understanding of the covenant that was cut on that tree 2,000 years ago.

I received a revelation of the finished work of the cross after going through a few years of grueling defeat in attempting to accomplish my own righteousness.

My salvation experience was a dramatic one indeed. I was deeply bound by the consequences of sin and was literally ready to be committed to a mental institution. I was emotionally disturbed, addicted, confused, clothed in shame, and completely guilt ridden. God in His rich mercy revealed Himself to me through an Anglican pastor, Reverend Ron Hunt, and his prayer group in Mission, British Columbia, Canada. I will never forget that evening! I had heard the testimonies of a number of Anglicans who had personally met Jesus. What I loved the most was that each of them shared how Jesus washed away their sins and gave them a new life. They were filled with so much love – so much grace.

After the meeting, I went home, fell on my knees in my living room, and nervously asked Jesus to come into my life. I was afraid that maybe my heart was too evil for Him to desire me. My sins seemed to be so much worse than those who openly shared at the prayer meeting. What if I was beyond hope? What if I had crossed a line that disqualified me from receiving forgiveness of sins and this new life I heard about? I timidly prayed,

"Jesus, I probably am not saying this right, but I would sure like You to come into my heart and forgive my sins like You did for the people at the prayer meeting."

Jesus did not hesitate. I literally felt Him enter my heart and remove my sin. All the tangible weight of my guilt and shame were gone in a moment of time. His presence felt like liquid love entering me. Jesus was not ashamed to call me His own.

I was now born again! I knew it! The entire night I wept with deep gratitude and joy. It was hard to believe that I was perfectly loved, accepted, and forgiven even though I had been so messed up. I had not done anything to deserve this. It was His gift of life and love to me. It was free. He paid the debt I could not pay. I immediately loved Him in return – how could I not? My life was truly changed. A miracle had taken place!

Following that experience, I sought the Lord with all my heart. Every moment was absorbed in thinking about Him and reading my Bible. I loved being in His presence and seeking Him through His Word. I served Him with all my heart – not because I had to but because love compelled me. I repented from everything He convicted me of – not because I was striving within myself to perfect my faith but because love filled me. I found myself hating what He hated and loving what He loved. I was saved!

This work of grace continued in my life, and every day I rejoiced in the goodness of the Lord. God was indeed at work within me, both to will and to do for His good pleasure (Philippians 2:13). I lived in Christ's deep peace and rest...UNTIL...I went to the mission field a few years later.

I only knew the grace and unconditional love of God. I had no idea that there was a legalistic demon that lurked in churches, ministries, and mission fields, attempting to destroy the wellbeing and faith of God's dear children. The leaders that had mentored me up to that moment were examples of love and grace, so I did not have a clue about religious spirits that tempted you to achieve your right standing with God through your own vain efforts. It was on the mission field where I went to serve the Lord in the advancement of His love Kingdom that I was introduced to these demons who pressured you to live by "the letter that kills" (see 2 Corinthians 3:6).

The leaders in the ministry we served were fantastic people. They were full of zeal, passion and commitment to God and labored beyond the call of duty. To this day, I love and honor them. I am impressed with their commitment and love for the Lord. However, they were bound by legalism and had a theological understanding that in addition to your faith in Christ's power to save you, there was a grave responsibility to "fix" your own life to make it pleasing to God. On a regular basis, in official "accountability meetings" they would point out areas of my life that were upsetting the Lord and provoking Him to anger. I was undone at the thought of hurting Him. To this day I cannot remember what the issues were – they were that insignificant, but at the time seemed to threaten my eternal well-being.

My husband and I had sacrificed greatly to serve on the field. We had hardly any financial support but had raised it ourselves by working and saving before leaving for the field. On the mission field, we served for over 14 hours per day and only had one and a half days off in five months. We were focused and completely committed to God. There were no personal "perks" in this assignment. Yet, we were constantly reminded of how we were disappointing God. We were taught to gird up and work on the things that needed to be "fixed." Not understanding the workings of the demon of self-effort and legalism, we fully engaged in the self-fix-up assignment.

I failed terribly. I was devastated at the thought of disappointing and provoking to anger the God I loved so deeply. I wanted to please Him with all my heart, yet I was failing in my attempts to clean myself up enough to give Him pleasure. Before I knew it, I was completely bound by religious oppression. I no longer felt the presence of God. I no longer felt His love and favor. I only wanted to please Him – but everything I attempted fell short. I felt condemned, guilt-ridden, and shame-filled. I was in a worse state than I was before I was born again! Self-righteousness and unrighteousness are equally evil.

We returned from the mission field beaten up. Our leaders at home took one look at us and realized what had happened. That is when we received our education on law versus grace. Our mentors taught us how religious spirits worked. It was great to understand the truth in our minds but it had not hit my heart yet. I daily struggled with self-condemnation as I did not fully grasp the finished work of the cross.

It was a few years later that I experienced a "God-encounter" that introduced me to the power of the cross. It is hard to explain, but in this amazing encounter I was shown by God the power of the finished work of the cross. The beloved Cross was the place where my God's love was tested. Jesus came to earth and suffered so much at the hands of sinful man. He faced everything that violated love – rejection, abandonment, betrayal, denial, slander, beatings, persecution, false accusations, theft and hatred. He passed every love test and it all culminated at the cross where He poured love out upon all mankind and decreed our remission of sins. "Father, forgive them for they know not what they do" (Luke 23:34 KJV). We were forgiven before we ever repented. After He forgave us, He gave up the ghost and became our sin. In exchange, He filled us with His righteousness. He paid the full price for our sin so that we would experience the perfect, unconditional love of God for all eternity.

When I finally received the revelation – not just in my mind but in my heart, I wept for days. I still weep when I am reminded of not only the price of His love for us but the eternal impact – what a gift!

You and I are safe and secure in His love forever. When we receive Jesus, we receive love, forgiveness, and life. Oh, how glorious! I do not understand individuals who claim to be Christians but still deliberately desire to sin. They could not possibly be saved yet with those desires, or perhaps they have greatly fallen away. When you have His love revealed to you, there is a new focus – a heavenly, righteous one. God-life rules you when you receive this glorious life. It is wonderful!

The greatest message, the greatest prophetic word, for all people and for all time is this: God loves you with an everlasting love – He really does! Living in The Zone is living in His love, and when you receive His love, you can love Him and others in return. "We love, because He first loved us" (1 John 4:19).

Make love your greatest aim in life. You have freely received and now you can freely give. There are many "grace-growers" and "love-growers" in your life that give you lots of opportunity to develop a mature love walk. Prophet Bob Jones died and was taken to heaven before being raised from the dead. When he stood before the Lord, he was asked one question, "Did you learn to love?" He had not, and the Lord sent him back.

I believe that the measure of our maturity in Christ is based on our love walk – not how much we know, how well we can prophesy, sing, or pray, but how well we love. If we have not love, it profits nothing (1 Corinthians 13). Heaven's atmosphere is love. I want to live in it and create an environment of love everywhere I go. To live in The Zone is to live in love. Let's do it!

FATHER'S LOVE LETTER

A Love Letter from Your Heavenly Father

My Dear Child,

I know everything about you. Psalm 139:1

I know when you sit down and when you rise up. Psalm 139:2

I am intimately acquainted with all your ways. Psalm 139:3

Even the very hairs on your head are numbered. Matthew 10:29-31

For you were made in My image. Genesis 1:27

I knew you even before you were conceived. Jeremiah 1:4-5

I chose you when I planned creation. Ephesians 1:11-12

You were not a mistake, for all your days are written in My book. Psalm 139:15-16

I determined the exact time of your birth and where you would live.
Acts 17:26

You are fearfully and wonderfully made. Psalm 139:14

I knit you together in your mother's womb. Psalm 139:13

And brought you forth on the day you were born. Psalm 71:6

It is My desire to lavish My love on you simply because you are My child and I am your Father. 1 John 3:1

I offer you more than your earthly father ever could. Matthew 7:11

For I am the perfect Father. Matthew 5:48

Every good gift that you receive comes from My hand. James 1:17

I am your provider and I meet all your needs. Matthew 6:31,32

My plan for your future has always been filled with hope. Jeremiah 29:11

And I rejoice over you with singing. Zephaniah 3:17

I will never stop doing good to you. Jeremiah 32:40

For you are My treasured possession. Exodus 19:5

I am your greatest encourager. 2 Thessalonians 2:16-17

I am also the Father who comforts you in all your troubles.
2 Corinthians 1:3-4

When you are brokenhearted, I am close to you. Psalm 34:18

As a shepherd carries a lamb, I have carried you close to My heart.
Isaiah 40:11

I am your Father, and I love you even as I love My Son, Jesus. John 17:23

I gave up everything I loved that I might gain your love. Romans 8:31-32

Nothing can ever separate you from My love. Romans 8:38-39

Because I truly do love you with an everlasting love. Jeremiah 31:3

With deep unwavering affection,

Your Heavenly Father

YOU ARE BLESSED WITH EVERLASTING LOVE

(Adapted from Father's Love Letter. Used by permission. Father Heart Communications Copyright 1999-2009 www.FathersLoveLetter.com)

DECREE – LOVE

My God loves me with an everlasting love that will never diminish or fade. His love towards me is perfect and it cannot fail. With lovingkindness He draws me to His heart. God's love is patient and kind. His love bears all things, believes all things, hopes all things and endures all things.

He loved me so much that He sent His only begotten Son to die on the cross for my sins. Because of this I have everlasting life and will never perish. As a result of God's great love for me I have an eternal, unbreakable covenant with Him. Everything He gave to Jesus, He has given to me because He loves me so deeply. He has withheld no good thing from me.

Through His covenant of love He has put His laws within my heart and written His commandments upon my mind. He created a banner of love over me and invited me to His banqueting table to feast in His presence.

I am rooted and grounded in His love and am able to comprehend its width, length, depth, and height. I am called to know His rich love that surpasses knowledge so that I may be filled with all the fullness of God.

Nothing can separate me from the love of God that is in Christ Jesus my Lord – not tribulation, or distress, not persecution, famine or nakedness; not peril, sword, angels, principalities, powers, death, or life; neither things present not things to come. Absolutely nothing can separate me from the love of God, which is in Christ Jesus my Lord. My life is filled with His love.

SCRIPTURES – LOVE

May he kiss me with the kisses of his mouth! For your love is better than wine. Your oils have a pleasing fragrance, Your name is like purified oil; Therefore the maidens love you. Draw me after you and let us run together! The king has brought me into his chambers. We will rejoice in you and be glad; We will extol your love more than wine. Rightly do they love you. Song of Solomon 1:2-4

He has brought me to his banquet hall, And his banner over me is love. Song of Solomon 2:4

The LORD appeared to him from afar, saying, "I have loved you with an everlasting love; Therefore I have drawn you with lovingkindness." Jeremiah 31:3

"Teacher, which is the great commandment in the Law?" And He said to him, " 'YOU SHALL LOVE THE LORD YOUR GOD WITH ALL YOUR HEART, AND WITH ALL YOUR SOUL, AND WITH ALL YOUR MIND.' This is the great and foremost commandment. The second is like it, 'YOU SHALL LOVE YOUR NEIGHBOR AS YOURSELF.' On these two commandments depend the whole Law and the Prophets." Matthew 22:36-40

For God so loved the world, that He gave His only begotten Son, that whoever believes in Him shall not perish, but have eternal life. John 3:16

"A new commandment I give to you, that you love one another, even as I have loved you, that you also love one another. By this all men will know that you are My disciples, if you have love for one another." John 13:34,35

Just as the Father has loved Me, I have also loved you; abide in My love. John 15:9

And hope does not disappoint, because the love of God has been poured out within our hearts through the Holy Spirit who was given to us. Romans 5:5

But God demonstrates His own love toward us, in that while we were yet sinners, Christ died for us. Romans 5:8

For I am convinced that neither death, nor life, nor angels, nor principalities, nor things present, nor things to come, nor powers, nor height, nor depth, nor any other created thing, will be able to separate us from the love of God, which is in Christ Jesus our Lord. Romans 8:38,39

If I speak with the tongues of men and of angels, but do not have love, I have become a noisy gong or a clanging cymbal. If I have the gift of prophecy, and know all mysteries and all knowledge; and if I have all faith, so as to remove mountains, but do not have love, I am nothing.

And if I give all my possessions to feed the poor, and if I surrender my body to be burned, but do not have love, it profits me nothing.

Love is patient, love is kind and is not jealous; love does not brag and is not arrogant, does not act unbecomingly; it does not seek its own, is not provoked, does not take into account a wrong suffered, does not rejoice in unrighteousness, but rejoices with the truth; bears all things, believes all things, hopes all things, endures all things.

Love never fails; but if there are gifts of prophecy, they will be done away; if there are tongues, they will cease; if there is knowledge, it will be done away. 1 Corinthians 13:1-8

See how great a love the Father has bestowed on us, that we would be called children of God; and such we are. 1 John 3:1

THE BENEDICTION

I know that when I come to you,
I will come in the fullness of the blessing of Christ.
Romans 15:29

BLESSED TO BE A BLESSING

Abraham's call to be blessed and to be a blessing is also our mandate today. Those who live in The Zone are blessed and commissioned to be a blessing to others. You cannot bless if you are not blessed. Receive the blessing. Establish your life in the Blessing Zone. Set your blessing perimeters and then go and bless everyone you can find.

Look for opportunities to fill the earth with God's goodness and bless as many people as you can in some way each and every day. Sow blessings in abundance. Make it a lifestyle.

Why? Because you can!

Why? Because you were created for this purpose!

Imagine what the world would be like if every Christian living in The Zone poured out blessings in their sphere of influence every day. The world would be an awesome place to live and the blessing model would catch on – a Blessing Revolution would erupt! Perhaps you will start such a revolution in your region. It only takes a spark to get a fire going.

You have freely received of the goodness of the Lord, so freely give. This is life in The Zone! The Apostle Paul understood this as he wrote to the church at Rome. He had freely received the blessing of grace and the fullness of the Kingdom of God. As a result, he was determined to visit them in the fullness of Christ in order to impart blessings to them. "I know that when I come to you, I will come in the fullness of the blessing of Chris " Romans 15:29

As I wrap up this message, I want to impart a blessing to you. I want you blessed beyond measure. I want you to live in the blessings of God in all that you are and in everything you put your hands to. The following benediction is God appointed. He instructed the priests (we are now the royal priesthood) to proclaim this blessing over the people of Israel. He said that once it was proclaimed, He would then bless them.

Then the LORD spoke to Moses, saying, "Speak to Aaron and to his sons, saying, 'Thus you shall bless the sons of Israel. You shall say to them: The LORD bless you, and keep you; The LORD make His face shine on you, and be gracious to you; the LORD lift up His countenance on you, And give you peace.' So they shall invoke My name on the sons of Israel, and I then will bless them" (Numbers 6:22-27).

THE BENEDICTION

Today you have a faithful, eternal, High Priest, Jesus Christ, who has secured the Father's perpetual blessing to each and every one who is in Him. In His name, I proclaim the following benediction over you in love and faith according to the instruction in the Scripture. I want you to receive the blessing into your spirit with boldness and confidence because from this time forward, you are being upgraded to life in the blessing zone. You will shift into accelerated measures of Christ's goodness. I believe it!

The Lord bless you.

The Lord keep you.

The Lord make His face shine on you.

The Lord be gracious to you.

The Lord lift His countenance on you.

The Lord give you peace.

Now...

Be Blessed!

Be a Blessing!

And...live in The Zone!

APPENDIX

PROPHETIC DECREE
~FAVOR~

Through Graham Cooke
May 2009

While ministering at a meeting in Pennsylvania, Graham Cooke brought forth by the inspiration of the Spirit of God this amazing prophetic decree. The room was charged with life, hope and faith. This word is not isolated to only those in attendance that evening. This word is for you!

A GREAT MOMENT OF FAVOR

This is a great moment for you. This is about favor and it's about vengeance. Let's just wait for a moment.

Father, I thank You. Holy Spirit, You are such a genius at life, and I know right now You are rubbing your hands with glee. I want to say to all who hear this word, this is your moment to turn the tables on the enemy, to live the life of *instead.* So, Father, we just wait.

HOLY SPIRIT IS BROODING

I want you to sense the Holy Spirit brooding over you. Is this too good to be true? You betcha, it's the good news. Does He border on fantasy? You betcha, it's the gospel. Glad tidings of great joy, heaven has come *instead* of hell, Jesus has come *instead* of the devil. You can have the life you always wanted, *instead* of the life you have always had – *instead*. That is possible because of the absolute, incredible, incomparable favor of God.

So I declare to you in Jesus' name, you have entered this evening. I am not prophesying something that is to come, but something that is here and now present. You are in it. God has created an atmosphere in your heart, in your life, where now the favor of God lives as a tangible reality. You are going to discover in these next days, weeks, months and years, the power of that favor. The power of moving in the opposite Spirit, that God grants you things *instead* of what the enemy would purpose. God is an alternative for you to have *instead*. And it is rooted in the favor of God.

UNPRECEDENTED, UNPARALLELED, FAVOR

And so I declare to you in the name of Jesus by the authority that God has given me as a prophet in the kingdom. I declare to you: This day marks the beginning of a life of unprecedented, unparalleled favor of God. That the favor of God is upon you right now, even as I speak. That you are going to learn to bask in that favor, to think in that favor, to live in that favor, to see from that place of favor, to move out in that place of favor, to proclaim rather than to pray. To proclaim favor upon yourself, favor in your circumstances.

You are going to learn how to fight in favor so that you may get vengeance. You are going to learn how to overcome, you are going to learn how to be more than a conqueror. You are going to see the goodness of the Lord in the land of the living, you are going to see the goodness of God in such ways that are unprecedented, unparalleled, that everyone around you will notice there is something different about you, there is something on you, there is something happening. What happened to you? What changed in you?

APPENDIX

AN ALTERNATIVE LIFESTYLE

And you are going to say, I have learned an alternative lifestyle *instead* of the one I had, I have learned an alternative lifestyle, I am a different person. I am not living that life, I am living a different one, I have the favor of the Lord. So I declare to you in Jesus' name, this is a time and a season of unprecedented, unparalleled favor of God that has come upon you.

God's favor will stay with you and will remain with you all the days of your life. You will abide in this favor because I have sent My Holy Spirit to teach you how to stay, to teach you how to dwell, to teach you how to remain, to teach you how to focus, to teach you how to pray, to teach you how to see, to teach you how to speak, to teach you how to walk and how to move, and how to live and how to have your being in My Son.

This is the favor of God upon your life and it will never go away. It is eternal, it is everlasting to everlasting, it is an eternal favor, it has no timeframe on it, it has no timeframe on it, it has no timeframe on it. It has begun now, and it will stay with you forever and ever and ever because it is everlasting, because I am your favor, I am your favor.

It's Me, it's Me, says the Lord. I am your favor, I have always been your favor, I will always be your favor, I am the *instead*, I am your *instead*, I am your promise, I am your prophesy, I am your blessing, I am *instead*, I am your *instead*. I am, I am your *instead*. I am, I am, My presence shall go with you.

FAVOR IS WRAPPED AROUND YOU LIKE A CLOAK

I am with you, I will never leave you nor forsake you and My favor is wrapped around you like a cloak. It is in your breath, it is in your lungs, it is in your heart. Every thought you have will be wrapped in favor. Every word you speak will bring favor to somebody. You will be favorable because you are highly favored. The favor of God is on you and it will never leave you.

So I say to you, says the Lord, trade on My favor, trade on My favor. Do not look at Me as though I am reluctant to bless you. I am extravagant, test Me, I am extravagant, and I am teaching you how to move from measure to fullness, how to live in abundance. I will teach you how to live in a place of abundance that's beyond your ability to think. You will need to dream, you will need to use your imagination, just to keep on conceiving about the goodness of the Lord and how strong it is and how powerful it is.

There is no place of despair because you live in the land of blessing, you live in the land of goodness—it is your inheritance. I am your inheritance, I am your territory, I am your promised land, I am your Canaan. I will give you houses you didn't build, I will give you vineyards you did not plant, to drink from wells you never had to dig. I am your inheritance, this is your day, this is your time. But you must take advantage of the goodness of God.

Beloved, this is not a concept, it is a tangible reality and you must now step into that place. You must cross that Jordan, you must enter into this space, you must occupy this place of favor until I come, because this is never-ending. And so says the Lord, I challenge you, I challenge you. I challenge you to believe, I challenge you to live, I challenge you to face everything in favor. I challenge you to position yourself before Me in every situation, in every circumstance.

A LIFE OF *INSTEAD*

There is always an *instead*, there is always an *instead*. And I am teaching you a life that is lived from heaven rather than from earth, *instead*. I am your *instead* and you have entered this place and now I am teaching you the joy of staying, dwelling, abiding.

Every problem, every bill, every situation, every circumstance, there is an alternative, *instead*. Beloved, it is important for Me, says the Lord, that you learn to live in My fullness, because the more fullness you draw from

Me – the more fullness I will have to give you, because what works for you, it works for you because it works for Me. I give and it is given back to Me. It works for you because it works for Me.

Pull favor out of Me and more favor will come. Pull favor out of Me and glory will come back to Me. So I challenge you, pull favor out of Me, pull favor down into your circumstances. I touch your eyes this evening and I give you a prophetic ability to see in the Spirit to see the opposite, to move in the opposite, to turn your problem into a prophesy, to turn your passivity into a promise. I give you an anointing to see the way I see and to speak the way I speak.

Bankrupt Me If You Can

And beloved, I am so challenging you. Come after Me, come after Me, bankrupt Me if you can. Listen, I need, I need My people living in abundance, I need it, I need it. I don't have a budget. The enemy has a budget, I have abundance. I need you to flow in the abundance of heaven. It is critical to what we are doing on the earth. It is critical that you become a people of abundance, of fullness, of favor, that you know how to get revenge, so you will learn to be more than conquerors, you will learn to be overcomers.

There are high places available here, beloved, come up, come up, come up. This is the year of your rising, this is the year of your rising. This is the year when you become untethered and unfettered. This is the year when impossible things will begin to occur around you because you are living in the power of *instead*. So I say to you, make a covenant with Me even as I have made a covenant with you. Make a covenant with Me, that you will follow through and partner with My Holy Spirit in these days. That you and I would have the pleasure together of working through your list. And know that we shall enjoy ourselves with you as we teach you to be unfettered, unbound, untethered, and you shall have your freedom.

You Shall Live In a Place of High Favor

You shall rejoice and you shall become worshippers. Your very life, your very breath will glorify Me. This is My will. My will is your *instead*, I am your *instead*. Make a covenant with Me even as I make a covenant with you for your good, to do you good, to do you good. That you would live in the goodness of the Lord, that you would overcome evil with all the good that I intend *instead*. And that you, beloved, shall live in a place of high favor and high renown and that you should have your vengeance, you should have your vengeance.

Father, we pray, we say amen, we say yes to You, Lord. I am in, I am in, I am tired of this life, I want another one *instead*. I am in, Lord, for Jesus' sake and for His honor, that He may look back on the travail of His soul and be satisfied. This is what He saw, this was the joy that was set before Him. His people, living in a difference place, *instead*. So, Father, we say yes to You, for the sake of Jesus and for His honor and glory. Amen.

Scripture Meditations For

LIFE IN THE BLESSING ZONE

God blessed them; and God said to them, "Be fruitful and multiply, and fill the earth, and subdue it; and rule over the fish of the sea and over the birds of the sky and over every living thing that moves on the earth." Genesis 1:28

And I will make you a great nation, And I will bless you, And make your name great; And so you shall be a blessing. Genesis 12:2

But you shall serve the LORD your God, and He will bless your bread and your water; and I will remove sickness from your midst. Exodus 23:25

"The LORD bless you, and keep you; The LORD make His face shine on you, And be gracious to you; The LORD lift up His countenance on you, And give you peace." Numbers 6:24-26

May the LORD, the God of your fathers, increase you a thousand-fold more than you are and bless you, just as He has promised you! Deuteronomy 1:11

He will love you and bless you and multiply you; He will also bless the fruit of your womb and the fruit of your ground, your grain and your new wine and your oil, the increase of your herd and the young of your flock, in the land which He swore to your forefathers to give you. Deuteronomy 7:13

However, there will be no poor among you, since the LORD will surely bless you in the land which the LORD your God is giving you as an inheritance to possess. Deuteronomy 15:4

For the LORD your God will bless you as He has promised you, and you will lend to many nations, but you will not borrow; and you will rule over many nations, but they will not rule over you. Deuteronomy 15:6

All these blessings will come upon you and overtake you if you obey the LORD your God: Deuteronomy 28:2

The LORD will open for you His good storehouse, the heavens, to give rain to your land in its season and to bless all the work of your hand; and you shall lend to many nations, but you shall not borrow. Deuteronomy 28:12

Now Jabez called on the God of Israel, saying, "Oh that You would bless me indeed and enlarge my border, and that Your hand might be with me, and that You would keep me from harm that it may not pain me!" And God granted him what he requested. 1 Chronicles 4:10

How blessed is the man who does not walk in the counsel of the wicked, Nor stand in the path of sinners, Nor sit in the seat of scoffers! But his delight is in the law of the LORD, And in His law he meditates day and night. He will be like a tree firmly planted by streams of water, Which yields its fruit in its season And its leaf does not wither; And in whatever he does, he prospers. Psalm 1:1-3

For You meet him with the blessings of good things; You set a crown of fine gold on his head. Psalm 21:3

The LORD will give strength to His people; The LORD will bless His people with peace. Psalm 29:11

O taste and see that the LORD is good; How blessed is the man who takes refuge in Him! Psalm 34:8

How blessed is he who considers the helpless; The LORD will deliver him in a day of trouble. The LORD will protect him and keep him alive, And he shall be called blessed upon the earth; And do not give him over to the desire of his enemies. Psalm 41:1,2

How blessed is the one whom You choose and bring near to You to dwell in Your courts. We will be satisfied with the goodness of Your house, Your holy temple. Psalm 65:4

How blessed are those who keep justice, Who practice righteousness at all times! Psalm 106:3

Praise the LORD! How blessed is the man who fears the LORD, Who greatly delights in His commandments. His descendants will be mighty on earth; The generation of the upright will be blessed. Psalm 112:1,2

The LORD bless you from Zion, And may you see the prosperity of Jerusalem all the days of your life. Psalm 128:5

May the LORD bless you from Zion, He who made heaven and earth. Psalm 134:3

Blessings are on the head of the righteous, But the mouth of the wicked conceals violence. Proverbs 10:6

It is the blessing of the LORD that makes rich, And He adds no sorrow to it. Proverbs 10:22

He who gives attention to the word will find good, And blessed is he who trusts in the LORD. Proverbs 16:20

A faithful man will abound with blessings, But he who makes haste to be rich will not go unpunished. Proverbs 28:20

"Bring the whole tithe into the storehouse, so that there may be food in My house, and test Me now in this," says the LORD of hosts, "if I will not open for you the windows of heaven and pour out for you a blessing until it overflows." Malachi 3:10

The thief comes only to steal and kill and destroy; I came that they may have life, and have it abundantly. John 10:10

Blessed be the God and Father of our Lord Jesus Christ, who has blessed us with every spiritual blessing in the heavenly places in Christ. Ephesians 1:3

But one who looks intently at the perfect law, the law of liberty, and abides by it, not having become a forgetful hearer but an effectual doer, this man will be blessed in what he does. James 1:25

Grace and peace be multiplied to you in the knowledge of God and of Jesus our Lord; seeing that His divine power has granted to us everything pertaining to life and godliness, through the true knowledge of Him who called us by His own glory and excellence. For by these He has granted to us His precious and magnificent promises, so that by them you may become partakers of the divine nature, having escaped the corruption that is in the world by lust. 2 Peter 1:2-4

Patricia King

Patricia is president of both Extreme Prophetic and Christian Services Association. She has been a pioneering voice in ministry, with over 30 years of background as a Christian minister in conference speaking, prophetic service, church leadership, and television & radio appearances. Patricia has written numerous books, produced many CDs and DVDs, hosts Extreme Prophetic TV, and is the CEO of a popular online media network – XPmedia.com. Patricia's reputation in the Christian community is world-renowned.

Christian Services Association (CSA) was founded in Canada in 1973 and in the USA in 1984. It is the parent ministry of Extreme Prophetic, a 501-C3 founded in 2004 in Arizona. CSA/Extreme Prophetic is located in Maricopa, AZ and Kelowna, B.C. Patricia King and numerous team members equip the body of Christ in the gifts of the Spirit, prophetic ministry, intercession, and evangelism. CSA/Extreme Prophetic is called to spreading the gospel through media.

Author Contact Information

Extreme Prophetic/CSA
U.S. Ministry Center
P.O. Box 1017
Maricopa, AZ 85139

XP Canada Ministry Center
3054 Springfield Road
Kelowna, BC V1X 1A5
CANADA

Telephone: 1-250-765-9286
E-mail: info@XPmedia.com

Join the Spiritual Revolution!

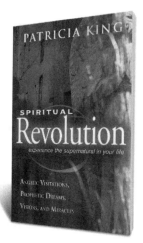

This book will shake the way you think about the supernatural power of God – and your role in combatting the counterfeit signs and wonders of today's cults. This books contains stories, insights and practical suggestions about how you can aggressively choose to live in the supernatural power of God.

Enlist in the *Spiritual Revolution* and you will be transformed into a powerful witness throughout an eternal lifetime!

Experience the God Kind of Love!

This booklet is designed to introduce you to the greatest revelation anyone could ever receive. It is the revelation of God's unconditional love for you – the love that was perfectly tested and proven at the cross 2,000 years ago.

It was never God's desire for you to experience rejection or abandonment. You were made to be a recipient of His bountiful grace and favor. Drink deeply of this revelation and come to the full realization that: *God Loves You with an Everlasting Love!*

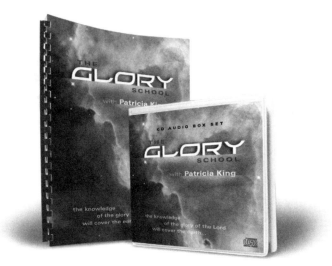

Additional copies of this book and other book titles from Patricia King, Extreme Prophetic and XP Publishing are available at **XPmedia.com**

BULK ORDERS: We have bulk/wholesale prices for stores and ministries. Please contact usaresource@xpmedia.com or 480-262-6405 and the resource manager will help you. For Canadian Bulk Orders please email resource@xpmedia.com or call 250-765-9286.

www.XPpublishing.com

A Ministry of Patricia King and Christian Services Association